Faith
THAT ALWAYS
WINS

DISCOVER THE POWER
OF A LIVING FAITH

FATAI KASALI

Faith THAT ALWAYS WINS

Copyright © 2016 Fatai Kasali

The author has asserted his right to be identified as the author of this work in accordance with the Copyright, Designs and Patents Act 1988.

All rights reserved. No part of this publication may be reproduced, stored in a retrieval system, or transmitted, in any form or by any means, electronic, mechanical, photocopying, recording or otherwise without the prior permission of the author.

All Scripture quotations, unless otherwise indicated, are taken from the Holy Bible, King James Version, Cambridge University Press, Oxford University Press, Harper Collins and the Queen's Printers.

Published in the United Kingdom, by Glory Publishing.

ISBN: 978-0-9926138-7-7

Acknowledgements

To God be the glory for the grace to write this book. I give God all the praise and adoration for giving me the inspiration through His Spirit. He has made the writing of this book possible.

My wife, Felicia Ebunlomo, gave me priceless support during the writing of this book. My two sons, Daniel and David, have also been very supportive.

To all those who have contributed in one way or another to the beauty of this work, thank you very much. May God Almighty bless you all.

Introduction

Faith has been described as *"the substance of things hoped for, the evidence of things not seen"* (HEBREWS 11:1). That is, faith is the foundation on which all our hopes and convictions for the future are built. The confidence that our unseen expectations shall be established is based on faith. This implies that the number of God's blessings a believer will be able to access in his or her lifetime depends on faith. Therefore, it is not surprising that the word 'faith' appears in several places in the Bible as a sign of its importance in the life of a believer.

This book explores the dynamism of faith and how it can be applied to various issues of life. You will learn in this book; how you can grow your faith to a level in which you become undefeatable in life. It is revealed in this book that faith has different stages of development, and this explains why some believers pass through life with failure and defeat. Every believer has a certain amount of faith at the beginning of their journey as a Christian. This was given in order to kick-start their journey, but it is not the end – it is the beginning. As you feed your spirit with the Word of God and grow in your knowledge of God, your faith level will grow. As you grow in faith, you will be able to trust God for greater miracles.

Furthermore, this book will teach you how to make your faith work for you as you face different situations of life. You will learn different strategies, as revealed in the Bible, of applying faith to deal with your confrontations.

You will discover, through this book, the attributes of faith. This will enable you to check whether you are genuinely operating in faith or not. Faith has attributes, and wherever it is in operation these are clearly revealed. It is one thing to say you are acting in faith; it is another thing to actually be acting in faith in a biblical way. Faith has its own nature, and if this is absent in any circumstances, such a believer is not acting in faith.

It is my hope that by the time you finish reading this book, your faith will have significantly grown.

Contents

1. Types of Faith 9
2. The Living Faith 15
3. Evidence of Things Not Seen 23
4. From Faith to Faith 31
5. Faith is a Mystery 51
6. Making Your Faith Work 67
7. Enemies of Faith 77
8. Making the Word Work for You 91
9. The Voice of Dominion 101
10. Using Your Faith to Defeat Hopeless Situations 113
11. Using Your Faith to Win Where Others Have Failed 121
12. Releasing the Creative Power of Faith into Action 133
13. Attributes of Faith 143

Types of Faith

CHAPTER 1

> *"Now faith is the substance of things hoped for, the evidence of things not seen."*
>
> HEBREWS 11:1

The word 'substance' in this definition of faith is a Greek word called *'Hupostasis'*. Hupostasis means 'stand under', that is, to be a foundation. This implies that faith is the foundation on which all our hopes for the future are built.

Also, the word 'evidence' suggests that faith is the conviction or persuasion of the existence of things that are not yet seen.

This definition of faith in HEBREWS 11:1 implies that faith is the foundation on which our conviction concerning the unseen but settled expectations for the future is based.

The reality of faith, based on the above definition, is that every human being has faith. We all demonstrate hope that our future expectations will be fulfilled. Whether we believe in God or not does not negate the fact that we have faith in something or somebody. This indicates that there must be a different kind of faith, since there are different sources of faith.

THE POWER FACTOR

Faith requires power if the fruit of faith is to be manifested. A man who has faith in something or somebody must believe that the something or somebody has enough power to meet his expectations. The source of the power enabling the faith to get results will determine the kind of faith in action. The strength of that power will also determine whether the expectations of those who have faith in that power will be fulfilled.

TYPES OF FAITH

There are basically three major types of faith. These are: natural faith, demonic supernatural faith and divine supernatural faith.

1. Natural faith

This is the type of faith dictated by nature or the experience of people. For example, based on experience, people have faith that the time of summer or winter, or rain or harmattan (dry season), will come. They look into the future based on their experience of the past, trusting that a certain season will soon come along. Similarly, people have faith that a pregnant woman will deliver the baby around nine months after conception. Experience has taught people to exercise such faith.

Furthermore, some people have faith in themselves or a fellow human being based on experience, especially past achievements. For example, some people believe strongly that they will always succeed in an examination because they have never failed in any past examinations. This makes such people have faith in themselves. There are also some people who put their faith in fellow human beings because of the past assistance they have enjoyed from them.

It is not a sin to exercise natural faith to a certain degree; it's just common sense. But you must acknowledge that the power behind its operation is from God.

Types of Faith

DEUTERONOMY 8:18 says: *"But thou shalt remember the LORD thy God: for it is he that giveth thee power to get wealth, that he may establish his covenant which he sware unto thy fathers, as it is this day."*

The power that makes a man succeed in life is from God. It is God who enables you to succeed. It is also God who enables another man to help you.

In DANIEL 2:20-21, Daniel said: *"Blessed be the name of God for ever and ever: for wisdom and might are his: and he changeth the times and the seasons: he removeth kings, and setteth up kings: he giveth wisdom unto the wise, and knowledge to them that know understanding..."*

It is God who set in motion all the seasons and natural patterns in life. It is God who set the time frame for different seasons. It is also God who determined that a human pregnancy normally takes nine months. The power behind its operation therefore is from God.

2. Supernatural Faith

The word supernatural combines two words: super (beyond) and natural (of nature). So something supernatural is that which does not conform to the natural or normal. This means that the situation can't be explained by known natural or human laws.

Supernatural faith is based on a spiritual source as its power.

There are two types of supernatural faith:

A. Demonic supernatural faith

The demonic supernatural controls demonic faith. It is under the control of the kingdom of darkness. This kind of power emanates from Satan, the head of the demonic kingdom. Some people put their faith in Satan as a source of fulfilment of their future expectations. Such people put their trust in the power of Satan. It is a demonic faith. For example:

> *"And Moses and Aaron went in unto Pharaoh, and they did so as the LORD had commanded: and Aaron cast down his rod before Pharaoh, and before his servants, and it became a serpent. Then Pharaoh also called the wise men and the sorcerers: now the magicians of Egypt, they also did in like manner with their enchantments. For they cast down every man his rod, and they became serpents: but Aaron's rod swallowed up their rods."* EXODUS 7:10-12

In these verses, Pharaoh and the wise men of Egypt had faith in the demonic supernatural. They worshipped Satan and put their trust in his power, whether they knew him by that name or not (Egypt's gods were satanic deceptions). All their future expectations were in Satan.

In this scenario, there is no human law or science that can explain how a rod can turn to snake. But those who believed in the power of Satan put their trust in Satan. They believed that when they called upon their gods to do something, their gods would do as they expected. To prove that Satan's power exists, their rods turned into snakes. However, what took place next proved the limitation of such power when those who put their faith in God come into operation: Aaron's rod ate up all the snakes of the Egyptian sorcerers!

B. Divine supernatural faith

The divine supernatural controls living faith – faith in God.

The divine supernatural is under the control of the kingdom of God. This kind of power emanates from God. Faith in God is called a living faith.

In the Old Testament of the Bible, before the birth of Jesus, Israel related with God as the God of Abraham, Isaac and Jacob. They exercised their faith in God through what they knew of God's dealings with Abraham, Jacob and Isaac. This was acceptable during that dispensation.

Exodus 3:15 says: *"And God said moreover unto Moses, Thus shalt thou say unto the children of Israel, the LORD God of your fathers, the God of Abraham, the God of Isaac, and the God of Jacob, hath sent me unto you: this is my name for ever, and this is my memorial unto all generations."*

In this verse, God introduced Himself to Israel as the God of Abraham, Isaac and Jacob. Their faith in God was exercised through this channel – the covenant God had made with these three ancestors. Whenever they reminded God of His covenant with Abraham, Isaac and Jacob, and kept their side of that covenant, they experienced the wonders of God. Their faith worked for them.

But in the New Testament of the Bible, after the birth, life, death, resurrection and ascension of Jesus Christ, faith in God can now only be exercised through Jesus Christ, His one and only Son. It is a new dispensation.

John 3:16 says: *"For God so loved the world, that he gave his only begotten Son, that whosoever believeth in him should not perish, but have everlasting life."*

It is only through Jesus Christ that you can exercise genuine faith. Any trust you put in anything outside Jesus can never attract the power of God.

This book is written to give you more knowledge of how you can exercise faith in Jesus Christ to win in life. Through the name of Jesus Christ, your faith will always attract the power of God into action to bring into existence all your expectations – if those expectations are in line with the Word of God.

The Living Faith

CHAPTER 2

"Jesus saith unto him, I am the way, the truth, and the life: no man cometh unto the Father, but by me."

JOHN 14:6

Faith in Jesus Christ is a living faith and also a saving faith. It is a living faith because it can grow and enable you to achieve greater success in your Christian journey. It is a saving faith because, by exercising it, it will save you from every work of Satan, including all the attacks and challenges of life. It will also bring you enlightenment and a change of lifestyle and destination. If you can master faith in Jesus Christ, you will see yourself winning and reigning in the spiritual life.

FACTS ABOUT THE LIVING FAITH

The following facts form a basic understanding that you must be aware of in order to benefit from exercising living faith over the issues of your life:

1. You must be born again

"Jesus answered and said unto him, Verily, verily, I say unto thee, except a man be born again, he cannot see the kingdom of God."
JOHN 3:3

To be born again means that you have been regenerated. You are a member of the kingdom of God through Jesus Christ. You can't exercise faith in God without being born again.

When you are born again, you receive the Holy Spirit, who lives inside you to empower you to operate beyond the natural or human level.

2. *The Word of God must dwell in you*

> *"It is the spirit that quickeneth; the flesh profiteth nothing: the words that I speak unto you, they are spirit, and they are life."* JOHN 6:63

The Word of God has spiritual power because it is inspired by the Holy Spirit – it is no ordinary book. You must store the Word of God in your spirit and ask the Holy Spirit to speak to you through it.

3. *You must obey the Word of God*

> *"My sheep hear my voice, and I know them, and they follow me…"* JOHN 10:27

You must live a life of obedience to the Word of God. You must be a 'doer' of the Word of God, not just a hearer.

4. *Jesus is the only way*

> *"Jesus saith unto him, I am the way, the truth, and the life: no man cometh unto the Father, but by me."* John 14:6

The only way you can set the power of God into motion in your life is through Jesus Christ. If you mingle anything outside Jesus into your faith in God, it will not attract the power of God.

Jesus is the only way to reach God and the only way to receive the Holy Spirit. For example, if you approach God in the name of Jesus but you still have confidence in the power of man or self or Satan, there will be no result.

5. Only the name of Jesus can work

> *"That at the name of Jesus every knee should bow, of things in heaven, and things in earth, and things under the earth..."* PHILIPPIANS 2:10

To set the power of God into motion, you have come to him in the name of Jesus, otherwise, there will be no response from God.

6. Apply the blood of Jesus

> *"Having therefore, brethren, boldness to enter into the holiest by the blood of Jesus."* HEBREWS 10:19

The shed blood of Jesus is one of the essential ingredients in a living faith.

In exercising your faith in God, you must believe in the efficacy – the effectiveness – of the blood of Jesus. The blood of Jesus is applied by faith by those who follow Jesus Christ.

7. Levels of a living faith

> *"For I say, through the grace given unto me, to every man that is among you, not to think of himself more highly than he ought to think; but to think soberly, according as God hath dealt to every man the measure of faith."* ROMANS 12:3

Each Christian has a different measure of living faith, as we are all different. But this faith can grow. It has an initial level when we are first converted, and it can advance from one level to the next level. The faith of a new convert is not expected to be greater than that of an 'old convert' who has seen and experienced the miraculous move of God in different situations of life. These different levels, and different kinds of faith, are described in the Bible.

A. *Beginner's faith*

> *"But as many as received him, to them gave he power to become the sons of God, even to them that believe on his name..."* JOHN 1:12

Beginner's faith is the faith of a person who has just accepted Jesus Christ as his or her Lord and is born again – a new convert. It is a faith that believes the Gospel and is what we are given at the beginning of the Christian journey.

B. *Mustard seed faith*

> *"And Jesus said unto them, Because of your unbelief: for verily I say unto you, if ye have faith as a grain of mustard seed, ye shall say unto this mountain, remove hence to yonder place; and it shall remove; and nothing shall be impossible unto you."* MATTHEW 17:20

The mustard seed was one of the smallest seeds known in Israel at Jesus' time. Mustard seed faith is the faith that has not grown much from the initial size when the Christian was born again. f

The mustard seed faith is still effective and can produce results, but it is just the beginning in the journey of living faith. No Christian is expected to fall below this level.

C. *Little faith*

> *"Wherefore, if God so clothe the grass of the field, which today is, and tomorrow is cast into the oven, shall he not much more clothe you, O ye of little faith? Therefore take no thought, saying, What shall we eat? or, What shall we drink? or, Wherewithal shall we be clothed?"* MATTHEW 6:30-31

This is a kind of faith that still worries about insignificant things of life such as material needs.

It is a sign of little faith to start worrying about things that unbelievers also worry about, such as what to eat or wear. Little faith worries about what God has already settled. It is a little faith to worry about what God has already provided for you.

D. Great faith

> *"The centurion answered and said, Lord, I am not worthy that thou shouldest come under my roof: but speak the word only, and my servant shall be healed. For I am a man under authority, having soldiers under me: and I say to this man, Go, and he goeth; and to another, Come, and he cometh; and to my servant, Do this, and he doeth it. When Jesus heard it, he marvelled, and said to them that followed, Verily I say unto you, I have not found so great faith, no, not in Israel."* MATTHEW 8:8-10

Great faith is the kind of faith that is fully persuaded about the Word of God. Such faith is confident, because God has spoken. It rests totally on the promises of God. This kind of faith is limitless in power because it functions based on the spoken Word of God.

The centurion had confidence in the spoken word of Jesus. He believed that what Jesus said was enough for him to experience the miraculous. Due to his faith in Jesus, who is the Word of God (JOHN 1:1), he experienced the miraculous. The spoken word of Jesus healed his sick servant.

E. Growing faith

> *"And the apostles said unto the Lord, Increase our faith."* LUKE 17:5

In this Bible verse, Jesus' disciples asked him to increase their faith. They had faith before this request, but they noticed certain challenges that their present faith could not handle – so they needed more.

Faith can grow and it can keep on changing.

Your faith must keep on growing, otherwise you will not be able to trust God in certain difficulties of life. For example, you can tell that you are growing in faith if you used to trust God for certain minor provision, but now you have advanced in your trust in God and you can now trust Him for something spectacular. Your faith is growing if yesterday you trusted God for healing for a minor sickness, but today you are trusting God to heal you of incurable sickness.

F. Shaking faith

> *"Now when John had heard in the prison the works of Christ, he sent two of his disciples, and said unto him, Art thou he that should come, or do we look for another?"* MATTHEW 11:2-3

This is a faith that is shaken by new or greater challenges. This is due to the fact that a person's faith has not been growing as expected. Unless you keep on growing in faith, you may find yourself lacking in faith when you face new or fresh challenges in life.

In the above story, John the Baptist, who introduced Jesus as his fore-runner in MATTHEW 3, is doubting if Jesus is the real Messiah Israel has been expecting. Perhaps John had certain expectations of Jesus that hadn't materialised. Maybe he expected Jesus to save him from his imprisonment. But for whatever reason, John had started doubting that Jesus was the Messiah. His faith in Jesus was shaking.

A faith that starts doubting God's faithfulness because He has not answered prayers or disappointed us in other ways, is a shaking faith. Such faith has not developed beyond the circumstances of life. A faith that functions only on what it can receive from God is not yet fully developed.

In DANIEL 3:16-18, Shadrach, Meshach, and Abednego's faith went beyond what they would receive from God. They said to King

Nebuchadnezzar: *"If it be so, our God whom we serve is able to deliver us from the burning fiery furnace, and he will deliver us out of thine hand, O king. But if not, be it known unto thee, O king, that we will not serve thy gods, nor worship the golden image which thou hast set up."*

The three Hebrews trusted God whether He saved them from the flames or not. If God intervened in their situation, fine; and if God didn't, it was still fine with them. To them, God was good irrespective of the way He chose to respond to their situation. God always honours such faith – a faith that has gone beyond receiving from God to the level of a trusting relationship. Such faith prefers that the will of God be done in their situation rather than their own will.

G. Faith as a gift of the Holy Spirit

All faith is a gift from God, but there is a special gift of faith that is one of the gifts of the Spirit listed in 1 CORINTHIANS 12:4-11.

A gift is what you receive due to the generosity of the giver. It has got nothing to do with your ability. Faith could be given as a gift by God to a certain individual or group to perform special tasks that are beyond the natural ability of the receivers. This kind of faith is given to the receiver for a moment and does not permanently rest on the person. God gives it to people to perform a task that is beyond their natural level of faith. When this gift is deposited in you, you may find yourself operating at an unusual level of faith for a moment.

For example, you may see yourself raising a dead person back to life, probably for the first time in your life. It is also possible for you to find yourself exercising unusual boldness to save somebody from danger. Usually after the task has been achieved, your faith level returns to its normal level. It has been a gift of faith, operating through you, and not your natural level of faith.

One example of this gift in operation is in ACTS 3:6-8: *"Then Peter said, Silver and gold have I none; but such as I have give I thee: In the name of Jesus Christ of Nazareth rise up and walk. And he took him by the right hand, and lifted him up: and immediately his feet and ankle bones received strength. And he leaping up stood, and walked, and entered with them into the temple, walking, and leaping, and praising God."*

This is the gift of faith in operation, not the natural level of faith of Peter. God gave this gift to Peter to glorify His name. It is possible for you also to receive such a gift if you can put Jesus first in your life and trust God to fill you with His Spirit. That will make you a candidate for the gift of faith, so that God will supernaturally enable you to perform certain tasks that will glorify His name.

Evidence of Things Not Seen

CHAPTER 3

"Now faith is the substance of things hoped for, the evidence of things not seen."

HEBREWS 11:1.

This verse defines what faith is. 'Substance' is the confidence you have in what you are expecting God to do. The strength of your confidence will be determined by the magnitude and reliability of the evidence. The kind of evidence that supports faith is not material evidence but spiritual. Faith in God is supernatural. It is a spiritual exercise not a human enterprise.

1 CORINTHIANS 2:12 says: *"Now we have received, not the spirit of the world, but the spirit which is of God; that we might know the things that are freely given to us of God."*

It is the Spirit of God who reveals to us the evidence to support our faith in God. It is the Spirit of God who dwells in us that gives us conviction as regards faith.

Faith can be described in a simple form as confidence that God will perform what He has promised. That confidence comes from the evidence we see that God does keep His promises. A lot of this evidence is seen in the Word of God, but also in the world around us, coupled with our experience of walking with God. Taken together, these prove beyond doubt that God will carry out what He has promised through His Word.

Examples of such evidence are:

1. God has integrity

> *"For all the promises of God in him are yea, and in him Amen, unto the glory of God by us."* 2 CORINTHIANS 1:20

Integrity means that His 'yes' will be 'yes' and His 'no' will be 'no'. He keeps His promises to us. He is honest and true. He does not change His promises. Whatever He promises to do concerning your situation, He will do.

NUMBERS 23:19 says: *"God is not a man, that he should lie; neither the son of man, that he should repent: hath he said, and shall he not do it? or hath he spoken, and shall he not make it good?"*

That is, the promise of God is sure and certain.

This is supportive evidence that should strengthen your faith in God. Since He does not lie or break His promises, then your part is to stand on such promises until there is fulfilment.

2. God is the creator

> *"In the beginning God created the heaven and the earth."* GENESIS 1:1

God brought all things into existence from nothing. He is the author of creation.

COLOSSIANS 1:16-17 says: *"For by him were all things created, that are in heaven, and that are in earth, visible and invisible, whether they be thrones, or dominions, or principalities, or powers: all things were created by him, and for him: And he is before all things, and by him all things consist."*

God created everything that exists, including powers, thrones and authority, both visible and invisible. He also upholds them by His power. The only thing He didn't create is evil, but He has power over evil. Therefore, He can control all things as it pleases Him. So, when you put your faith in God, you are putting your faith in somebody who owns all things – both visible and invisible – and is in control.

3. God has already given His best

> *"He that spared not his own Son, but delivered him up for us all, how shall he not with him also freely give us all things?"* ROMANS 8:32

The best gift any human being could ever request from God is His Son, Jesus Christ. If God can give you His only begotten Son to die for your sin, is there anything too big that He can't give you? There is nothing else you can request from God that can be bigger than Jesus Christ. If He can give you Jesus, He can give you anything.

4. God has unlimited ability

> *"For with God nothing shall be impossible."* LUKE 1:37

> *"I know that thou canst do every thing, and that no thought can be withholden from thee."* JOB 42:2

The ability of the person promising you a gift will determine the level of confidence you can place in his promises. We can see from the above verses that God is all-powerful – able to do all things. There is nothing you can ask from God that is impossible for Him to do (apart from commit sin). That is another evidence to strengthen your confidence in God as you exercise your faith in Him.

5. God is the source of all good things

> *"John answered and said, A man can receive nothing, except it be given him from heaven."* JOHN 3:27

If you know that what you are seeking is available from the person you are asking, then you know that there is at least a possibility that you can receive it. There would be no point in asking if the person didn't have what you want. In God's case, all good things are found in Him, so if you ask Him for anything good, you know you have come to the right source.

JAMES 1:17 says: *"Every good gift and every perfect gift is from above, and cometh down from the Father of lights, with whom is no variableness, neither shadow of turning."*

It is God who gives good things. When you exercise faith in God to supply you certain good things and there seems to be a delay, this is not due to the unavailability of what you are requesting. If you can keep on asking, the answer will come. All the good things you need for life are in God.

6. God rewards faith

> *"But without faith it is impossible to please him: for he that cometh to God must believe that he is, and that he is a rewarder of them that diligently seek him."* HEBREWS 11:6

Whenever you exercise faith in God, a reward is certain and sure. God likes people approaching Him for help.

> *"And I say unto you, Ask, and it shall be given you; seek, and ye shall find; knock, and it shall be opened unto you. For every one that asketh receiveth; and he that seeketh findeth; and to him that knocketh it shall be opened."* LUKE 11:9-10

Whoever approaches God in faith for blessing will not be disappointed. This is another piece of evidence on which you can base your faith in God.

7. God honours His Word

> *"I will worship toward thy holy temple, and praise thy name for thy lovingkindness and for thy truth: for thou hast magnified thy word above all thy name."* PSALM 138:2

God does not disregard His Word. Whenever you approach God to fulfil His Word in your situation, God will honour your request.

God has magnified His Word above His name. He has respect for His Word. This is another part of the evidence that your faith will be rewarded in the way in which Scripture promises. It builds your confidence to know that the person you are asking to fulfil his promise will not ignore what he has promised.

8. God is love

> *"He that loveth not knoweth not God; for God is love."* 1 JOHN 4:8

God loves you and He will never ignore your cry for help. The evidence of His love towards you gives you confidence whenever you exercise faith in God. Because He loves you, He will not hesitate in fulfilling His promises in your life.

The love God has for you is unconditional, which means that His love towards you does not depend on what you are like or what you have done. He loved you before you came into existence. This should give you confidence that whatever you ask God for, will be provided because He loves you.

9. God rules in the affairs of life

> *"But God is the judge: he putteth down one, and setteth up another."*
> PSALM 75:7

God is the ultimate judge who rules over the affairs of life. He has final say over all the matters of life. If you approach God because your case needs the intervention of a higher authority, then you can be sure that He is in charge. God is the judge of all judges. When He is on your side, you can never lose a case, no matter how bad it is.

God is the judge. He decides who should be set free or imprisoned. He also decides who should be promoted or demoted.

DANIEL 4:17 says: *"This matter is by the decree of the watchers, and the demand by the word of the holy ones: to the intent that the living may know that the most High ruleth in the kingdom of men, and giveth it to whomsoever he will, and setteth up over it the basest of men."*

God rules in the affairs of men. God has the final word on what happens to us all.

ISAIAH 46:10 adds: *"Declaring the end from the beginning, and from ancient times the things that are not yet done, saying, My counsel shall stand, and I will do all my pleasure…"*

Whatever God decides on, will be done. His judgement is final. This gives confidence when you find yourself experiencing injustice in life, since you already have the judge of the universe on your side. God is the real judge.

10. God never changes

> *"Jesus Christ the same yesterday, and today, and for ever."* HEBREWS 13:8

> *"For I am the LORD, I change not; therefore ye sons of Jacob are not consumed."* MALACHI 3:6.

What God has done in the past, He will do again, because He never changes. If you have received a miracle from God in the past, that is evidence that He will do it again, because you know He can do it again.

God's character does not change. His attributes remain the same. His ability remains the same. He does not depreciate, neither in personality nor in power.

PSALM 77:11 says: *"I will remember the works of the LORD: surely I will remember thy wonders of old."*

Like the psalmist, we can look at what God has done in the past as a guide to the future. The miracles God has already done in your life are part of the evidence that God will not disappoint you.

From Faith to Faith

CHAPTER 4

> *"We are bound to thank God always for you, brethren, as it is meet, because that your faith groweth exceedingly, and the charity of every one of you all toward each other aboundeth."*
> 2 Thessalonians 1:3

This verse shows that faith can grow. Faith is dynamic. Faith in God should not be static. God wants your faith to grow. He wants you to move from beginner's faith to great faith.

Growing in faith is an evidence of maturity in the Christian journey. At the beginning of your journey, you might have started by trusting God for small things such as your daily needs. That is fine. But after walking with God a while, you should be able to trust Him for something bigger, something more spectacular.

You started your Christian journey by being able to trust God for His blessings, but after some time you should start trusting God to make you a blessing to others. God wants you to experience the deeper things of heaven while you are on earth. Unless you grow in faith, it will be difficult for you to experience the bigger things of God. Unless you move from one degree of faith to the next, it will be difficult for you to move from blessing to blessing.

HOW TO GROW IN FAITH

If you are to grow in faith, you will need to practise the following on a regular basis:

1. Increase your knowledge of God

> *"And now, brethren, I commend you to God, and to the word of his grace, which is able to build you up, and to give you an inheritance among all them which are sanctified."* ACTS 20:32

The more you know about God, the more your faith in Him will grow, and the better you know God, the better you will be able to exercise greater trust in His power. By studying the word of God regularly, you will discover how God operates and how He reacts to the faith of His children. Through His Word (the Bible), you will discover how to attract God's attention to your situation. You will also discover the secrets of faith in God.

It is the Word of God that builds up faith in God. By reading His Word, you will discover how people of the past experienced mighty works of God through faith. This will not only strengthen your faith but also equip you with the knowledge that will enable you to know what to do and how to act, in order to see the wonders of God in your situation.

Paul declared that he knew the one he believed in and this strengthened his faith: *"For the which cause I also suffer these things: nevertheless I am not ashamed: for I know whom I have believed, and am persuaded that he is able to keep that which I have committed unto him against that day"* (2 TIMOTHY 1:12.

2. Create an atmosphere of faith around yourself

> *"So then faith cometh by hearing, and hearing by the word of God."* ROMANS 10:17

What you see and hear regularly will influence what you think. What you think will in turn influence what you say and do. So, it is important that you surround yourself with an atmosphere that promotes faith.

For example, regularly listening to the Word of God, whether spoken or sung, will affect your thinking and re-programme the way you think. It will increase your faith.

Surround yourself with songs and hymns that promote faith. Surround yourself with pictures and texts that promote faith. Similarly, surround yourself with people who will promote your faith. Avoid discussing your life issues with people that have no word of faith in them. Don't involve people who speak wrong words in the affairs of your life. Don't listen to just any word of advice or counsel. Not everybody should speak into your life. Some people carry words of impossibility; don't give them the chance to speak into your situations.

3. Speak your faith

> *"We having the same spirit of faith, according as it is written, I believed, and therefore have I spoken; we also believe, and therefore speak."*
> 2 CORINTHIANS 4:13

As a Christian, you must know that your words significantly shape your life. It is important that you always speak words of faith from the Bible into your situation. Make yourself an addicted speaker of the word of faith.

Speak what you expect God to do concerning your situation. Speak what the Word of God says about your situation. Speak what you believe that God is able to do concerning your situation. Always be a speaker of the word of faith. By doing this, you will train your tongue to always speak words of faith. This will take you from faith to more faith. You will soon see yourself exercising faith in all situations.

4. Act your faith

"Even so faith, if it hath not works, is dead, being alone." JAMES 2:17

Put words into action. Don't stop at speaking the words of faith, but advance by putting the words of faith into practice in your life.

Take a step of faith concerning your situation. Faith without any corresponding actions is dead.

For example, if you believe that God can heal you of paralysis, occasionally make an effort to walk out of your wheelchair. If you believe that God is able to provide you with a job, start seeking information about job vacancies and make applications.

5. Pray for faith

"And the apostles said unto the Lord, Increase our faith." LUKE 17:5

It is true that you don't need to pray for faith because, as a believer, you have already been given faith. But God can help you to increase what you already have. He will help you to grow in faith if you ask Him. Through prayer, God can remove barriers that are hindering your faith. It is also possible for God to supernaturally enable you to exercise faith beyond your normal ability.

In MARK 9:24, we read that *"the father of the child cried out, and said with tears, Lord, I believe; help thou mine unbelief."*

God can help your unbelief and increase your faith. Regularly pray to God to help your faith to grow. Ask Him to help you to trust Him for greater things. God can do it for you.

6. Get rid of fear

"There is no fear in love; but perfect love casteth out fear: because fear hath torment. He that feareth is not made perfect in love."
1 JOHN 4:18

If there is fear in you, it will not allow your faith to grow. You must deal with fear. Fear is the opposite of faith. You must get rid of fear. Fear is of the devil. It's one of the weapons he uses to hinder our faith.

If God is love and there is no fear in love, then fear is not from God.

2 TIMOTHY 1:7 says: *"For God hath not given us the spirit of fear; but of power, and of love, and of a sound mind."*

If God has not given you the spirit of fear, then it must come from the devil or your own feelings. Therefore, never justify your fear, but confront it so that your faith in God can grow.

To deal with fear in your life, start walking in love towards everybody. Love everybody irrespective of their limitations or weaknesses. Avoid being judgemental, because it will hinder you from walking in love with people. Just love people, not because of who they are but because they are made in the image of God. Loving everybody will help you to be free whenever you are in the midst of people. It will also clear your mind of any guilt. This will enable your faith to grow.

PHILIPPIANS 4:6 says: *"Be careful for nothing; but in every thing by prayer and supplication with thanksgiving let your requests be made known unto God."*

This verse teaches that we should avoid anxiety and worry because they kill faith in God. Whenever you face challenges, what you need is God's intervention, not worry or anxiety. It is therefore wise to talk to God in prayer concerning what you need, and to avoid exhibiting anxiety that can't help your situation. Faith will only grow in an atmosphere of peace.

When the faith of disciples came under attack, they prayed to God for boldness: *"And now, Lord, behold their threatenings: and grant unto thy servants, that with all boldness they may speak thy word"* (ACTS 4:29). Boldness removes fear. This enables faith to grow. Pray regularly to God for boldness so that your faith can grow.

7. Be positive

> *"Run now, I pray thee, to meet her, and say unto her, Is it well with thee? is it well with thy husband? is it well with the child? And she answered, It is well..."* 2 KINGS 4:26

A mind filled with negativity will kill faith. Choose to be positive in life, irrespective of the prevailing circumstances around you. Choose to believe that with God all things are possible.

When you choose to be positive, you have not chosen to be unrealistic or delusional as some people claim. Being positive in God, even in an obviously negative situation, is a claim that you refuse to accept the opinion and position of the enemy (devil). Being positive indicates that, irrespective of the situation, you still believe that the supernatural reigns over the natural.

In 2 KINGS 4, the only child of the Shunammite woman died, but when the woman was asked by the servant of God about her child and the family, she replied that all was well. How could she say, *"It is well"* (4:26) when she had a dead child?

The woman was not being untruthful or delusional; she was declaring what she believed through God, irrespective of the prevailing situation. She chose to be positive. As a result, in 2 Kings 4:36, the child came back to life.

For your faith to grow, you must choose to be positive, regardless of what is happening around you. You must not allow the situation to dictate to you whether you should trust your God. Keep the faith even in a negative situation, because God is always bigger than the situation you see.

8. Go higher

> *"And whatsoever ye shall ask in my name, that will I do, that the Father may be glorified in the Son."* JOHN 14:13

To grow your faith, you will need to go higher in the nature of things you ask from God. You will remain at the same level of faith if your requests never change. You will need to start trusting God for something greater.

In the above verse, Jesus makes it clear that there is no limitation on what God expects you to ask from Him. Whatever you ask will be granted. Therefore, you will need to change your request if you want your faith to grow.

For example, if your prayer has been limited to 'God, please bless me' you can change it to 'God, please, make me a blessing'. It will require a greater commitment of faith to move from receiving blessings to being a distributor of blessings. This is how faith can grow. With greater demand comes greater faith.

9. Bear your suffering

> *"That the trial of your faith, being much more precious than of gold that perisheth, though it be tried with fire, might be found unto praise and honour and glory at the appearing of Jesus Christ..."*
> 1 PETER 1:7

God wants to help you increase your faith. In order to do this, God sometimes exposes His children to certain challenges that will mature their faith. Such challenges come with suffering and it will happen irrespective of your holiness or wisdom. You can't escape the suffering God has allowed you.

It usually comes through persecution, when you are busy doing the right things. Such suffering will come not because of any wrong things you have done. God allows it to grow your faith and to glorify His name. If you can bear that situation, you will come out better and stronger in faith.

The suffering that comes is allowed by God to test the genuineness of your faith and to refine it. If you patiently bear it, the name of God will be glorified and your faith will receive approval from God.

In 1 PETER 3:17 we read: *"For it is better, if the will of God be so, that ye suffer for well doing, than for evil doing."* And 2 TIMOTHY 3:12 says: *"Yea, and all that will live godly in Christ Jesus shall suffer persecution."*

These verses support the fact that God allows a certain amount of suffering in the lives of His children. It may come through persecution, in which you may be punished for an offence you did not commit. God allows it to test whether you will trust Him for your deliverance or not. If you react the wrong way to suffering, you will mess up your testimony as a child of God.

Furthermore, the suffering that comes your way may actually be allowed by God as chastisement. HEBREWS 12:6-8 says: *"For whom the Lord loveth he chasteneth, and scourgeth every son whom he receiveth. If ye endure chastening, God dealeth with you as with sons; for what son is he whom the father chasteneth not? But if ye be without chastisement, whereof all are partakers, then are ye bastards, and not sons."*

Sometimes, God uses suffering as a punishment for your wrongdoing – but His aim is always to correct you, not to harm you. Your faith will be strengthened if you bear the situation and maintain your trust in God. The chastisement is evidence that you are a child of God and He is at work in your life to make you more like Jesus. God is correcting you in love for a greater future that He has planned.

But be assured that in all these challenges, God will not allow you to face a situation you can't bear. That is why you will have no excuse for messing up your faith under suffering.

1 CORINTHIANS 10:13 says: *"There hath no temptation taken you but such as is common to man: but God is faithful, who will not suffer you to*

be tempted above that ye are able; but will with the temptation also make a way to escape, that ye may be able to bear it."

God will not expose you to challenges He knows you can't survive. At the end of your trial or chastisement, your faith will have grown and matured. Bear it; it is for your own good.

10. Hold on to past miracles

> "I will remember the works of the Lord: surely I will remember thy wonders of old." PSALM 77:1

You can help your faith to grow if you remember the miracles of the past. What God has done for you before will strengthen your faith to believe Him for your present situation.

David strongly believed that the God who helped him to be victorious in the past would help him to be victorious in the present. He said: *"The LORD that delivered me out of the paw of the lion, and out of the paw of the bear, he will deliver me out of the hand of this Philistine"* (1 SAMUEL 17:37)

Past miracles strengthened David's faith in God. If God has done it before, He can do it again. If God has delivered you before, He can deliver you again. Every miracle is a stepping stone to trusting God for greater things.

11. Spiritual logic

> "And be not conformed to this world: but be ye transformed by the renewing of your mind, that ye may prove what is that good, and acceptable, and perfect, will of God." ROMANS 12:2

When you choose to have faith in God, the devil will attempt to attack your mind and influence you to reason yourself out of faith.

He may raise a series of questions in your mind that appear logical and reasonable to you, to make you argue yourself out of faith.

The solution to defeat this demonic logic of doubt is to practise spiritual logic. Spiritual logic is a way of reasoning from the Word of God, being adamant that, irrespective of the prevailing contradictory situation, God will do what He has promised and that He is able to still achieve His purpose. This kind of reasoning will increase your faith in the Lord, especially when it seems as if there is an obvious contradiction between what you see happening and what God has promised.

HEBREWS 11:17-19 says: *"By faith Abraham, when he was tried, offered up Isaac: and he that had received the promises offered up his only begotten son, of whom it was said, That in Isaac shall thy seed be called: accounting that God was able to raise him up, even from the dead; from whence also he received him in a figure."*

Abraham practiced spiritual logic. God had promised him that, through Isaac, he would have nations in his name. But the same God asked Abraham to sacrifice the same Isaac to him. The question was: how could Isaac have descendants that turn into nations if he was to be sacrificed to the Lord? The situation seemed to say that the initial promise of God to Abraham had been cancelled. But Abraham reasoned that even if Isaac died, God was still able to raise him from dead in order to keep His initial promise. This kind of logic quenches every reason that might negate our solid confidence in the promises of God.

In the same vein, if God has enabled you to start a project and suddenly you run out of resources, instead of believing the suggestion of the devil that the plan has collapsed, you can reason within yourself in this way: How could an all-sufficient God start a project that He would not be able to finish? Your answer will be no, it is impossible.

Furthermore, maybe God told you that He has healed you of a certain disease and yet you still feel its symptoms. In that case, instead of accepting the devil's suggestion that the sickness can't be healed, you can reason within yourself in this way: Can an all-powerful God surrender to sickness? Your answer will be no, it is impossible.

Through this kind of reasoning, you will be able to defeat any negative question the devil may bring to your mind to frustrate your faith in God. You will be able to overcome the contradictory situation you face.

12. Adjust your belief system

> *"And we know that all things work together for good to them that love God, to them who are the called according to his purpose."*
> ROMANS 8:28

You can grow in faith if you can adjust your belief system. It is true that you are a believer of God, but there is a certain set of silent beliefs in your heart that may influence how fast and how well your faith can grow.

For example, get it into your belief system that in all situations of your life God is always at the centre. The God that you trust in is never on holiday. He is always at the centre of your life's events, both good and bad, actively directing and monitoring the situation.

GENESIS 50:18-20 says: *"And his [Joseph's] brethren also went and fell down before his face; and they said, Behold, we be thy servants. And Joseph said unto them, Fear not: for am I in the place of God? But as for you, ye thought evil against me; but God meant it unto good, to bring to pass, as it is this day, to save much people alive."*

In this story, Joseph's brothers came to apologise to him for the evil they did to him by selling him into slavery in Genesis 37. To their surprise, Joseph did not punish them for selling him into slavery, but told them that God had allowed it to happen in order to promote His purpose for Joseph's life. This implies that Joseph saw God's hand at work behind the evil done to him, even though God himself did not and cannot do evil. To Joseph, if his suffering had not been part of God's plan, God would not have allowed it.

Your faith will rise when you have the internal conviction that God is at the centre of your situation, irrespective of whether it is good or bad.

A believer who wants to grow in faith must never accuse or blame God, or believe that God is absent from the situations of his life. The God that you believe in never sleeps nor takes the day off!

Furthermore, get your true identity in the Lord into your belief system. Your qualification to exercise authority over the situations of life is based on what Jesus has done for you, not on who you are. It is a gift, not something you can earn.

This belief will enable you to defeat the devil when he comes to attack your mind with guilt and condemnation, reminding you of your wrongdoing. Many Christians cannot grow in faith because they believe the lies of the devil concerning their position in the Lord. This demonic attack constantly brings them down, whenever they make an effort to rise in faith.

What qualifies you to exercise faith in God is the righteousness of Jesus Christ – not your own righteousness. ROMANS 3:22 says: *"Even the righteousness of God which is by faith of Jesus Christ unto all and upon all them that believe..."*

You are a son of God and you have the authority of God inside you, not because of your goodness but because of Jesus Christ. With more understanding of who you are in the Lord, you will lay claim to more of your inheritance in the kingdom of God and exercise more authority over situations in life.

Finally, you will need to believe in miracles for your faith to grow. Whenever you face difficult situations in life, tell yourself that a miracle can happen and that it will happen in your favour.

Faith in God is supernatural. It is not natural. It does not operate according to the rules of man. Get the possibility of miracles into your spirit. A miracle can't be explained by natural or scientific laws. When miracles happen, human reasoning is suspended. Therefore, for you to grow in faith, you must believe in miracles. You must believe that what appears negative can still become positive when it receives divine attention.

THE POWER OF REGULAR FASTING

> *"And Cornelius said, Four days ago I was fasting until this hour; and at the ninth hour I prayed in my house..."* ACTS 10:30

Fasting is an abstinence from food in order to have a better focus on prayer. As a believer, fasting can help you to grow in faith. This is because fasting helps you to subdue the flesh – our sinful nature – the major hindrance to faith.

A believer who regularly fasts and prays will be able to control the influence of the flesh. In many situations, believers can't exercise control over issues of their lives because of the flesh. The flesh promotes human reasoning that hinders release of faith.

In MATTHEW 17, Jesus' disciples could not heal a child tormented by a demon, despite having faith. When they asked Jesus why they could not do it, He answered that *"this kind goeth not out but by prayer and fasting"* (verse 21).

But He also told them that their faith was not strong enough (verse 20), so the implication is that such a miracle can only be done when faith is strengthened by prayer and fasting.

If you want to be a believer who can exercise control over the situations of life without any limitation, you will need to cultivate the habit of regular praying and fasting. It is true that you already have faith and it is also true that you already have the Word of God inside of you. But you will not be able to rule over all situations of life unless your faith grows to a certain level, and this will require regularly subjecting the flesh to your control through fasting.

If the flesh is unable to rise against your faith, the spiritual authority inside of you will rise above the hindrance of the flesh. If certain problems resist your command, introduce fasting. Set aside certain days that you will fast and pray, with the intention of strengthening your spirit. The power that prayer and fasting can generate in your spirit will amaze you.

SPEAKING IN TONGUES

> *"But ye, beloved, building up yourselves on your most holy faith, praying in the Holy Ghost..."* JUDE 1:20

Regularly speaking in tongues strengthens your spiritual nature. Your real self is inside. Your faith level is determined by what Paul calls your "inner man" or "inward man".

> *"That he would grant you, according to the riches of his glory, to be strengthened with might by his Spirit in the inner man."* EPHESIANS 3:16

> *"For which cause we faint not; but though our outward man perish, yet the inward man is renewed day by day."* 2 CORINTHIANS 4:16

Modern translations translate the "inner man" as "inner being" as it applies to all Christians – male or female.

If you can regularly speak in tongues, you will be able to make your inner being stronger and this will improve your faith level. Regular speaking in tongues, coupled with fasting and prayer, can renew your inner being: *"He that speaketh in an unknown tongue edifieth himself..."* (1 CORINTHIANS 14:4).

These are spiritual exercises that make your world cease to be ordinary. There is a faith that attracts blessings, but there is another level of faith that makes you a blessing to others. You can be spiritually empowered to such a level that miracles become a common experience in your life. But you will need to build up your inner being for this to happen.

WHY YOU MUST GROW IN FAITH

Growing in faith is mandatory for every believer for several reasons.

> *"Then touched he their eyes, saying, According to your faith be it unto you."* MATTHEW 9:29

This man was healed because of his faith. This implies that the degree to which we enjoy the blessings of God depends on our faith. Our holiness, obedience, love and other qualities also affect how successful our Christian lives will be, but faith is an important factor. The more you grow in faith, the more blessings you will be able to enjoy in the kingdom of God. The higher your faith, the higher will be the spiritual authority you will be able to exercise over the issues of life. Blessings will come according to your faith.

> *"If any of you lack wisdom, let him ask of God, that giveth to all men liberally, and upbraideth not; and it shall be given him. But let him ask in faith, nothing wavering. For he that wavereth is like a wave of the sea driven with the wind and tossed."* JAMES 1:5-6

This verse implies that answers to prayer depend on unwavering faith. It is very unlikely that you will seriously ask God for something that is beyond your level of faith. A man who has grown in faith will be able to trust God for greater things as he present them before God. It is one thing to pray; it is another thing to have faith that the prayer will be answered. If you want to ask God for spectacular things, you must develop your faith so that you will pray with faith.

> *"Above all, taking the shield of faith, wherewith ye shall be able to quench all the fiery darts of the wicked."* EPHESIANS 6:16

Your faith level matters in spiritual warfare. Faith is a shield that can defend you against the arrows of the enemy. But the strength of the shield will be determined by the level of your faith.

One arrow of the enemy is to attack the mind with deceptive statements and negative thoughts. You will need faith to be able to debunk all such lies. Unless your faith has grown, it may be difficult to clearly identify that some thoughts coming into your mind are actually from the devil. There are many believers who run away when they face challenges in life, because their faith level remains at the beginner's stage – just the same as when they first came to Christianity.

> *"But without faith it is impossible to please him: for he that cometh to God must believe that he is, and that he is a rewarder of them that diligently seek him."* HEBREWS 11:6

Nothing done before God without faith will be accepted by Him. Your prayer, worship, sacrifices and services will not receive favourable attention from God unless they are carried out in faith. The more faith you add to whatever you do before God, the more you will make God pleased with you. As your faith grows, you will be able to do greater things in the name of God, and this will bring greater pleasure to God and greater rewards from Him.

Your faith matters. For your faith to bring you greater rewards, it must grow from level to level. Desire to grow in faith today and you will be amazed how much reward you will bring into your life.

> *"For whatsoever is born of God overcometh the world: and this is the victory that overcometh the world, even our faith."* 1 JOHN 5:4

Jesus has made you victorious. He has made you an overcomer. Through his death, Jesus has given you the right to overcome every wicked act of the devil. But for you to live the life of an overcomer, you will need faith. We enjoy all that Jesus has done for us through faith, so the level of your faith will determine how much you will be able to enjoy what Jesus has done for you.

Through faith, you can rule over fear. Fear is the opposite of faith. As you face more threatening situations in life, you will need faith that has grown from level to level.

> *"Hearken, my beloved brethren, hath not God chosen the poor of this world rich in faith, and heirs of the kingdom which he hath promised to them that love him?"* JAMES 2:5

From this verse, it is clear that as a child of God, you have an inheritance in God – you are an heir of the kingdom. Your spiritual inheritance includes peace, joy, dominion, power, victory, etc. But you will need faith to fully enjoy all these. The more you grow in faith, the more you will be able to claim and enjoy your inheritance. If you are not growing in faith, you will be robbing yourself of so many spiritual blessings.

Furthermore, to enjoy the power of God will require faith. To enjoy the power of God in a greater dimension requires that you grow in faith.

> *"Verily, verily, I say unto you, he that believeth on me, the works that I do shall he do also; and greater works than these shall he do; because I go unto my Father."* JOHN 14:12

Unless you grow in faith, it will become impossible for you to set in motion the power of God.

We live in a world filled with fear and rumours of war. It is becoming increasingly difficult to live in our world these days without faith in God. For you to enjoy peace of mind, free from fear, you will need faith. The more you grow in faith, the more you will exhibit peace and rest of the mind.

> *"For we which have believed do enter into rest, as he said, As I have sworn in my wrath, if they shall enter into my rest: although the works were finished from the foundation of the world."* HEBREWS 4:3

Faith in God guarantees your rest and peace of the mind in this wicked world that is full of evil.

In many situations, you will need inner strength to resist the devil. He will attempt to lure you into sin and fear by creating circumstances that pressurise you or influence you. You will need faith to withstand his schemes.

> *"Submit yourselves therefore to God. Resist the devil, and he will flee from you."* JAMES 4:7

To resist the devil requires spiritual ability, not human effort. You will need faith to reject all the attacks of the devil, both internally and externally. As the devil increases his influence on you, you will need to match that with faith that increases too.

Finally, you must know that there are certain problems of life that only respond to faith. Such problems can't be resolved by any human solutions.

> *"Jesus answered and said unto them, Verily I say unto you, if ye have faith, and doubt not, ye shall not only do this which is done to the fig tree, but also if ye shall say unto this mountain, Be thou removed, and be thou cast into the sea; it shall be done."* MATTHEW 21:21

Mountains are problems of life that can't be solved by any human means. They are too mighty and they resist any solution unless it is spiritual. You will need faith to overcome such mountains. You will also need to grow in faith in order to overcome certain types of mountains. Some problems have deep roots that spring up from generation to generation. They will require great faith.

Faith is a Mystery
CHAPTER 5

"The secret things belong unto the LORD our God: but those things which are revealed belong unto us and to our children for ever, that we may do all the words of this law."

DEUTERONOMY 29:29

A mystery is something that is baffling – it defies understanding and cannot be explained. It beats human ingenuity and intelligence. God has certain mysteries – secrets kept from the understanding of men.

How faith works and produces the results promised in God's Word is one of those mysteries. Its operation is known only to almighty God and controlled by Him, who Himself is also a mystery!

The little we know about God is revealed through the Bible. There is no man who has detailed knowledge about the appearance of God or the way He works. God is a spirit and His ways are only known by Him. As ISAIAH 55:9 says, *"For as the heavens are higher than the earth, so are my ways higher than your ways, and my thoughts than your thoughts."*

These mysteries necessitate faith, because there are times when we must keep our faith in God even though we don't understand what He is doing.

Therefore, because faith in God is a mystery:

1. If you want to enjoy the blessings of faith, you must stop being natural both in thinking and expectations.

2. When you are operating in faith, you must know that your operating location has shifted from the natural to the supernatural. Faith takes you out of the natural world into the world of the supernatural. As you exercise your faith, you will be interacting with the unseen supernatural forces waiting to obey your word. So in matters of faith, your word matters.

3. When you are operating in faith, you must start using the conviction that nothing is impossible: *"For with God nothing shall be impossible"* (Luke 1:37). In the world of the supernatural, there is no impossibility. It is only in the natural world that there are impossibilities. There are many problems man has not been able to solve because man operates in the natural world.

4. If you are operating in faith, don't try to understand how it will happen. It is a waste of time to attempt to work out what you don't know. It is a mystery.

5. Faith takes the matter out of your control as a human being. When you set your faith in motion concerning certain things, the divine forces of the supernatural take over the matter from your hand. You can't be in control any more. Therefore, your human aspect will fail to help you in the matter.

6. In faith, anything human fails. For example, human wisdom, reasoning, logic, analysis and common sense will woefully fail when applied to faith. You can't operate in faith and still operate in human attributes.

7. In faith, the input does not determine the output. The word you speak in faith is intangible, but the result of that word when mixed with faith could be tangible. For example, the word God spoke in Genesis 1 was intangible, but the creatures that were created as a result were tangible.

The following are mysteries you must be aware-of, so that you can operate effectively in faith:

1. *Mystery of invasion*

When faith is released into action, the supernatural invades the natural, in both tangible and intangible ways. The forces of the supernatural are unseen but their actions can be clearly seen. We see the movement but we don't see the forces responsible for it. It is a mystery.

> *"For the children of Ammon and Moab stood up against the inhabitants of mount Seir, utterly to slay and destroy them: and when they had made an end of the inhabitants of Seir, every one helped to destroy another."*
> 2 CHRONICLES 20:23

In 2 Chronicles 20, Jehoshaphat and the people of Judah prayed to God for intervention against the allied force that came to attack them. It was a prayer of faith. The unseen forces of the supernatural invaded the army of Judah's enemies and the enemies started fighting each other. Their minds and reasoning were totally invaded and brought under full control of the unseen forces of the supernatural. This is a mystery.

Whenever you release your faith into motion over certain areas of your life, you will be inviting the unseen forces of God to invade the natural for your sake. For example, when people who once said no to your job application suddenly change their decision to yes, after you have prayed in faith, then you will know that there has been an invasion from the unseen forces of the supernatural.

2. Mystery of empowerment

Faith makes you stronger than you are. When you release your faith into certain areas of your life, you will be divinely empowered to perform beyond your natural ability. That is why, if you are operating in faith, never undermine yourself. This is because when the Spirit of God fills you, you will amaze yourself.

> *"And the hand of the LORD was on Elijah; and he girded up his loins, and ran before Ahab to the entrance of Jezreel."* 1 KINGS 18:46

King Ahab had set off in his chariot long before Elijah began running because rain was coming. Amazingly, Elijah, on foot, overtook Ahab. Where did Elijah get the strength from in order to run ahead of a chariot pulled by horses? This is a mystery, because normally a man cannot outrun a horse. But faith makes you stronger than you really are.

With faith in God, you can achieve far more than your natural abilities would normally allow. That is why you should not underrate yourself, neither should you believe the devil when he speaks to your mind, telling you that you don't have what it takes to succeed in certain areas of life. When you bring in faith, you can go far. Do not try to use your human reason to work out how far you can go, because when faith comes in, situations go beyond normal.

3. Mystery of the written Word of God

The Bible is the written Word of God, but that Word is not ordinary. While the Word of God is written in black and white in a form everybody can read, it is not an ordinary word. When it is mixed with faith, the Word of God can do all things.

Faith will require that you speak the Word of God into your situation, but you must know that the efficacy of that Word is beyond human understanding. While the Word of God may appear simple when you speak it, do not underestimate its power.

> *"It is the spirit that quickeneth; the flesh profiteth nothing: the words that I speak unto you, they are spirit, and they are life."* JOHN 6:63

The words of Jesus have spiritual power. They are no ordinary words. They are full of dynamic power that can do all things. Every single letter in the Word of God has got His Spirit behind it to make it supernatural in action. We see the letter but we don't see the Spirit behind it. It is a mystery.

> *"For the word of God is quick, and powerful, and sharper than any two-edged sword, piercing even to the dividing asunder of soul and spirit, and of the joints and marrow, and is a discerner of the thoughts and intents of the heart."* HEBREWS 4:12

The written Word of God can do all things. It is a mystery that by just releasing the written Word into a situation, things begin to change. Do not try to guess how the situation will turn out when you release the Word of God into it. Miracles are bound to happen whenever the Word of God is released into a situation, but not necessarily in the way we expect. It's God's Word and He fulfils it how He sees fit. It's a mystery.

4. *Mystery of a small god*

> *"I have said, Ye are gods; and all of you are children of the most High."* PSALM 82:6

The Word of God declares that you are a small god – a small version of the almighty God. It is not surprising – after all, the child of a dog is a dog. If you are a child of God, then you are also a god. That doesn't mean you have all the powers of God, because a child does not have all the powers of a parent. But whenever a child needs his parent, he can depend on all the power of the parent, because every good parent comes to his children's aid. And it does mean that you are made in God's likeness – in His image.

> *"And the LORD said unto Moses, See, I have made thee a god to Pharaoh: and Aaron thy brother shall be thy prophet."* EXODUS 7:1

In the story of the Exodus, God told Moses that He would make him seem like a god to his enemy, Pharaoh, because God would work through Moses. The mystery of being a small version of the almighty God is that you can operate on the same level as God when it comes to faith. You can exercise God-like faith, because faith comes from God.

> *"And God said, Let the waters bring forth abundantly the moving creature that hath life, and fowl that may fly above the earth in the open firmament of heaven. And God created great whales, and every living creature that moveth, which the waters brought forth abundantly, after their kind, and every winged fowl after his kind: and God saw that it was good."* GENESIS 1:20-21

God spoke into existence all the birds and sea creatures. He commanded the waters to produce living creatures and it was so. God just spoke. He did not debate the possibility of His Word bringing the results.

> *"And he turned back, and looked on them, and cursed them in the name of the LORD. And there came forth two she bears out of the wood, and tare forty and two children of them."* 2 KINGS 2:24

In this story in 2 KINGS, Elisha was mocked by a group of children and he placed a curse on them. His word caused two bears to come out of the wood and attack the children. This shows the power of the word of a man of faith. With God's kind of faith, man can speak things into existence. It is a mystery, but it works. As a believer, you must realise that you are a small version of almighty God and your tongue is anointed. You can speak things into existence with God-like faith. There is no point in trying to explain it or understand how it works, because we will never know this side of eternity.

5. *The mystery of no distance or time*

Faith is not limited by time or distance. If we get out of range of a mobile phone signal, the phone doesn't work. But faith has no such problems with working over vast distances. This is because, in faith, the supernatural rules, and the supernatural world is not restricted to physical distance or time. In eternity (the supernatural world is beyond time and space) the past, present and future co-exist.

> *"But, beloved, be not ignorant of this one thing, that one day is with the Lord as a thousand years, and a thousand years as one day."* 2 PETER 3:8

In heaven, the home of the supernatural, they don't count days because there is no darkness. They only have one day in heaven. Time does not exist there.

Therefore, when faith comes into action, there is no restriction. That is why it is possible for you to command situations happening thousands of miles away to change immediately. Your word does not need to travel for hours to reach a faraway location and be effective there. It is instantaneous.

> *"And Jesus said unto the centurion, Go thy way; and as thou hast believed, so be it done unto thee. And his servant was healed in the selfsame hour."* MATTHEW 8:13

The word of Jesus healed a servant at the same time the word was released. Distance did not count. Faith is of now.

With faith, the challenges of many years can disappear within minutes. You can change the situation in a faraway place just by exercising faith in the secret place of your room. There is no distance in faith. Your word of faith can go to places where you can't go physically.

6. *The mystery of creation*

Creation by God means to bring into existence from what is non-existent. That is, to use nothing to make something. In a human context, to bring anything into existence will require pre-existing materials and energy – the capacity to work. We can only make something out of something else. God can make something out of nothing.

In JOHN 6:11-13, Jesus prayed over five barley loaves and two small fishes and they multiplied to feed over 5,000 people. And there were twelve baskets of food left-over: *"And Jesus took the loaves; and when he had given thanks, he distributed to the disciples, and the disciples to them that were set down; and likewise of the fishes as much as they would. When they were filled, he said unto his disciples, Gather up the fragments that remain, that nothing be lost. Therefore they gathered them together, and filled twelve baskets with the fragments of the five barley loaves, which remained over and above unto them that had eaten."* It was faith in action.

The question is: where did the energy that turned the loaves and fish into abundance come from? It's a mystery. Only God knows.

Faith does not function based on human experience or skills. The supernatural functions on its own principles. When faith comes into operation, the anointing (heavenly power) is released into motion to act on the material under consideration. There is nothing the anointing can't do with any resource, irrespective of its size. That is why, when you are using your faith, believing that your little resources will receive multiplication, don't try to analyse it. How your little resources will multiply and serve your purpose is not subject to human experience and analysis.

The anointing has no limitation. It can work wonders, both in the life of man and any material. Heavenly energy is different from earthly energy. Once you release your faith into your situation, the heavenly anointing begins to move things around, causing all necessary changes that will birth your miracles. You don't need to see the movement, just believe it is happening in the realm of the spirit. It is a mystery.

7. *The mystery of obedience*

When faith is released, everything obeys – whether living or non-living. With faith, even the dead can obey. When faith is released into motion no created thing is immune to its power, irrespective of its location.

In MATTHEW 8:26-27, Jesus' followers were amazed to see that even the winds and the sea obey the command of Jesus Christ: *"And he saith unto them, Why are ye fearful, O ye of little faith? Then he arose, and rebuked the winds and the sea; and there was a great calm. But the men marvelled, saying, What manner of man is this, that even the winds and the sea obey him!"*

The disciples could not understand how sea and wind could obey the voice of a man.

> *"For by him were all things created, that are in heaven, and that are in earth, visible and invisible, whether they be thrones, or dominions, or principalities, or powers: all things were created by him, and for him..."* COLOSSIANS 1:16

This verse says that all things, whether physical or spiritual, were created by Jesus and for Jesus. When they hear the name of Jesus, they have to respond positively.

Likewise, PHILIPPIANS 2:10 does not make any distinction between living and non-living things: *"That at the name of Jesus every knee should bow, of things in heaven, and things in earth, and things under the earth..."* All must bow before Jesus. This means that even stones and water must respond to the name of Jesus. This is a mystery. In the realm of the spirit, everything is able to hear and respond to the name of Jesus.

The verses we've looked at in this chapter clearly indicate that the power of God resides in the word of your mouth as a believer, because we are the sons and daughters of God. It means that your word – if spoken in faith – rules over all situations. How far your word will go to generate influence on the situation is far beyond your experience and imagination.

8. *The mystery of interconnectivity*

Faith establishes a direct connection between yourself and the supernatural. That is why, when you start operating in faith, you should stop viewing situations from the point of view of the natural world where you are at the moment. It is a mystery that while you are here on earth, your faith is influencing things in the heavens above.

Due to this interconnectivity, faith enables you to access resources in the realm of the spirit. You can be here on earth and still cause resources to flow from heaven into your situations here on earth. Understanding this mystery will enable you to dwell in an abundant supply of good things here on earth.

But faith is closely connected to obedience. MALACHI 3:10 says: *"Bring ye all the tithes into the storehouse, that there may be meat in mine house, and prove me now herewith, saith the LORD of hosts, if I will not open you the windows of heaven, and pour you out a blessing, that there shall not be room enough to receive it."*

If you are obedient to God by practising the act of giving by faith, you will directly connect your finances to heaven, and this will cause a release of financial blessings into your life here on earth. How this will happen is beyond human explanation, but it will happen. When your act of faith ignites this kind of reaction in heaven you will notice increase that is beyond your understanding. It is because your act of obedient faith has connected your finances to heaven for supply.

THE PARADOX OF FAITH

> *"As it is written, I have made thee a father of many nations,) before him whom he believed, even God, who quickeneth the dead, and calleth those things which be not as though they were."* ROMANS 4:17

In faith, we call things which are not as if they were. We speak into existence what we desire. In faith, we speak the end at the beginning. In faith, we speak of what we foresee happening into the contradictory prevailing situation. In faith, we call beautiful the prevailing ugly situation. It is because that is our expectation. We superimpose the future on the present. This seems contradictory, but it is the principle that works in faith.

> *"Neither shall thy name any more be called Abram, but thy name shall be Abraham; for a father of many nations have I made thee."* GENESIS 17:5

Abraham had no descendants when God was referring to him as a father of many nations. God was calling a childless person the father of many children. This is contradictory to the prevailing situation in the life of Abraham. God was superimposing the future upon the present. Faith speaks its intention – it is not limited by the current situation. For example, if you are told by doctors that you have only a few days to live due to a terminal illness, you can begin to call yourself by what you see yourself becoming in many years to come. By faith you choose to focus on what you want your tomorrow to be, while you negate what the present is telling you.

> *"Run now, I pray thee, to meet her, and say unto her, Is it well with thee? is it well with thy husband? is it well with the child? And she answered, It is well."* 2 KINGS 4:26

As we saw in chapter 4, the Shunammite woman said it is well with her dead son. This is a contradiction. Eventually the dead son came alive, but when she said "it is well" the situation was far from well. Her confession of faith brought into existence the fruit of her faith.

Therefore, if you want your negative situation to change to positive, you will need to practise the paradox of faith. Never refer to your bad situation as being bad, rather keep on calling it what you want it to become and what you believe it will become. It is only a matter of time; the supernatural will respond to your word of faith. This is a holy contradiction. It works. It is a mystery.

Of course, there is one caveat. If what you are believing God for is not in line with God's will and Word, then no amount of faith will work. We can't have faith for something sinful or contrary to God's Word.

THE MIND FACTOR

> *"For who hath known the mind of the Lord, that he may instruct him? But we have the mind of Christ."* 1 CORINTHIANS 2:16

As a Christian, you have the mind of Christ. This is different from your natural mind. A Christian is expected to manifest and operate with the mind of Christ. It is a supernatural mind. It enables you to think and reason like Jesus.

When your confession of faith agrees with the thought of your mind, certain actions can be initiated in the spiritual realm. But in some situations, a confession of faith does not yield the expected result because there is a disparity between the thoughts in our head, or the feelings in our heart, and the word of confession on our lips.

MATTHEW 15:8-9 says: *"This people draweth nigh unto me with their mouth, and honoureth me with their lips; but their heart is far from me. But in vain they do worship me, teaching for doctrines the commandments of men."*

This indicates that, in some situations, confession is not matched by our thoughts and feelings. Jesus was saying that people can come to God and speak words of faith while their heart and mind reflect different things. In such a situation, the word of faith becomes ineffective. In your demonstration of faith, you must ensure that your thoughts agree with your action of faith, otherwise your faith will produce no result.

> *"And be not conformed to this world: but be ye transformed by the renewing of your mind, that ye may prove what is that good, and acceptable, and perfect, will of God."* ROMANS 12:2

This verse instructs us to renew our mind so that we can think in line with God's will. If your mind does not think faith when you speak faith into your situation, there will be no manifestation of the result you were expecting.

But if you entertain double-mindedness, your word of confession will betray you, as JAMES 1:5-8 says:

"If any of you lack wisdom, let him ask of God, that giveth to all men liberally, and upbraideth not; and it shall be given him. But let him ask in faith, nothing wavering. For he that wavereth is like a wave of the sea driven with the wind and tossed. For let not that man think that he shall receive any thing of the Lord. A double minded man is unstable in all his ways."

Double-mindedness is an enemy of faith. This is because double-mindedness means we harbour doubts that inhibit our faith. God sees our heart and knows our mind, so He will not honour a confession of faith on the lips if we are not sincere in our heart and convinced of the truth of the confession in our mind. For God to act in response to our faith we need to be single-minded, otherwise it is not really faith at all.

When you choose to verbalise the right thought, there will be no fruit if you also carry the wrong thought within you. If you have the thoughts of both possibility and impossibility in your heart and you choose to speak possibility into a situation, there will be no result. This is because the two thoughts contradict each other. For your confession of possibility to generate a result through verbalisation, you will need to get rid of the second thought of impossibility from your mind.

THE WAY OF THE SPIRIT

> *"For my thoughts are not your thoughts, neither are your ways my ways, saith the LORD."* ISAIAH 55:8

God is a spirit and His ways are spiritual. God is a mystery and His ways are mysterious. Man is natural but His God is supernatural.

To operate in faith will require that you understand that the way of the spirit is totally different from the way of the carnal (physical) man. Therefore, you will need to set aside your natural tendency to attempt to calculate the possible outcome of your faith and its operation. You will need to stop guessing what God is likely to do and how He is likely to act in your situation, based on your experience so far. God is the God of the unexpected.

Do not subject the ways of God to human analysis.

> *"Then Elisha said, Hear ye the word of the LORD; Thus saith the LORD, To morrow about this time shall a measure of fine flour be sold for a shekel, and two measures of barley for a shekel, in the gate of Samaria. Then a lord on whose hand the king leaned answered the man of God, and said, Behold, if the LORD would make windows in heaven, might this thing be? And he said, Behold, thou shalt see it with thine eyes, but shalt not eat thereof."* 2 KINGS 7:1-2

Faith is a Mystery

In this story, the servant of the king is saying that it is impossible that the Lord will make food become abundant within 24 hours, after many years of famine. This servant probably relied on his experience and natural knowledge to determine the possibility of this prophecy coming true. Probably he thought about what it would take to make food abundant in the land. First, you need farmers to plough their lands, then they would have to sow the seeds, and then wait for the rain for the seeds to germinate and grow to maturity. After all this, you can normally expect a harvest.

To this servant's mind, it would take weeks and months for farmers to get food ready for the villagers to buy and eat. Without God's intervention, he was right. But he failed to realise that there was so much he did not know about what God can do. He did not know that before God makes a promise, the fulfilment is ready in the realm of the spirit.

For your faith to bring you the results you expect, you will need to stop forecasting the possibility of those results and the method by which it may happen. Faith requires that you understand that it is all about mystery, not human experience and understanding.

Making Your Faith Work

———————————————————————— CHAPTER 6

> *"Thy word is a lamp unto my feet,*
> *and a light unto my path."*
>
> PSALM 119:105

As a believer, the seed of faith is already inside of you. But as you face situations of life, you will need to release your faith into action so that God can provide for your needs and achieve great things for His kingdom through you.

THE MIND OF GOD

The word of God stipulates the rules and principles of His operations, which guide us in most aspects of life, but for some decisions we need to seek the mind of God. In other words, there are times when the way ahead is not clear and we need to know what God wants us to do.

> *"And they put him in ward, that the mind of the LORD might be shewed them."* LEVITICUS 24:12

This verse shows that Moses sought God's will when there was a decision to make. His answer came in the following verses. For your faith to work, you will need to ensure that you know the mind of God concerning your situation. You will need to check what God says about that situation in His Word, and if you can't find anything specific, you need to seek God's guidance through prayer. Then you can put your faith to work.

You must be aware that your faith will not yield results if it works in contradiction to the Word of God. PSALM 119:105 says: *"Thy word is a lamp unto my feet, and a light unto my path."* In other words, the Bible is our guide for life. Check out what God says about that sickness you want to cure by faith. Check out what God says about that debt you are trusting God to sort out for you. Check out what God says about your problems.

Now that you have understanding about what God says concerning your situation, you can embark on the following exercises that will enable your faith to work for you:

1. Start from the victory side

Every coin has two sides: heads and tails. In every battle there are two sides: victory and defeat.

1 CORINTHIANS 15:57 confirms that you have been made victorious over every issue of life through Jesus Christ: *"But thanks be to God, which giveth us the victory through our Lord Jesus Christ."*

That is, your victory was settled over 2,000 years ago when Jesus came to die for you. Therefore, to make your faith work over the situations of your life, start from the victory side. Understand and believe that Jesus has won the battle for you! You were made victorious long before the present challenge of your life came into existence.

> *"And when he had consulted with the people, he appointed singers unto the LORD, and that should praise the beauty of holiness, as they went out before the army, and to say, Praise the LORD; for his mercy endureth for ever. And when they began to sing and to praise, the LORD set ambushments against the children of Ammon, Moab, and mount Seir, which were come against Judah; and they were smitten."*
> 2 CHRONICLES 20:21-22

In this story, Jehoshaphat taught us how to face a battle from the victory side. The people of Judah entered the battlefield singing, rejoicing and praising the Lord. They went into battle celebrating their victory, which God had given them before the battle even commenced. This set their faith in motion.

To make your faith work, face your situation from the victory side. Before you do anything about that situation, sing, rejoice and give God quality worship. In reality, you must know that God will only allow you to face the battle He has won for you through Jesus Christ. God expects you to enter every battle of your life from the victory side by celebration of who He is and what He has done for you.

2. Confess the Word

Speak into your situation with the promise of God in His Word for such a situation. You will need to continually speak the Word of God over that situation, irrespective of the prevailing circumstances around it. Keep on speaking the Word out both loudly and silently, as the situations around you permit.

For example, if you are facing incurable sickness, you can stand on the two Bible verses below and continually declare them to your sickness.

> *"I shall not die, but live, and declare the works of the LORD."*
> PSALM 118:17

Keep on telling yourself that you shall not die but live. This is your desire and not what the situation says. Therefore, keep on declaring your desire and not what the people or situation say.

> *"Who his own self bare our sins in his own body on the tree, that we, being dead to sins, should live unto righteousness: by whose stripes ye were healed."* 1 PETER 2:24

The Word of God says that by the stripes (wounds) of Jesus Christ you were healed. Keep on declaring to that sickness that you have been healed by the stripes of Jesus Christ. For example, tell that cancer that you have been healed of cancer many years ago (about 2,000 years ago when Jesus Christ came to die for you), and therefore cancer has no right to stay inside your body. It has to go in the name of Jesus. Irrespective of the prevailing situations, maintain your confession of faith.

3. Speak prophetically

In order to set your faith into motion, you can speak the Word of God prophetically to your situation. Prophetical utterances talk about what will soon happen. Through a prophetical utterance, you can determine the future occurrence of your situation; that is, what the present situation will turn out to be in future. By standing on the Word of God, you can instruct your tomorrow what it should be.

> *"And Moses said unto the people, Fear ye not, stand still, and see the salvation of the LORD, which he will shew to you to day: for the Egyptians whom ye have seen to day, ye shall see them again no more for ever."* EXODUS 14:13

In this verse, Moses spoke prophetically about what would become of the Egyptians who were chasing the people of Israel. He told Israel that they would see the Egyptians no more – because they would drown in the Red Sea. The question is: How did Moses know that this would happen? Moses had no idea what God would do or how He would save Israel from the Egyptians.

But Moses believed that God would not lead Israel out of Egypt just to allow the Egyptians to slaughter them by the Red Sea. Moses knew God had shown His love for them by taking them out of Egypt, so he chose to be positive that God would save them again. Moreover, the Spirit of God was upon Moses. He had the mind of

Christ that enabled him to reason as Jesus would do if he was in the same situation.

In speaking prophetically, you may not know how the situation will turn out, but you can still prophesy about it, based on the love and care of God that you know and have previously experienced. For example, at least you know that God loves you. With that conviction you can begin to prophesy what the loving God could do for you in your situation that would prove His love in your life. Because He loves you, He will not let you be put to shame. Therefore you can prophesy to the situation that seems as if it will bring you shame, that it will turn out to your honour.

4. Rule by decree

As a Christian you are a king; kings rule by decree.

REVELATION 1:6 says that Jesus *"hath made us kings and priests unto God and his Father; to him be glory and dominion for ever and ever. Amen."*

Jesus has made you a king and priest unto God. Ecclesiastes 8:4 says that the word of a king carries power: *"Where the word of a king is, there is power: and who may say unto him, What doest thou?"*

When you release your word into your situation, you set in motion the authority that will enforce your expectations regarding the situation. When you decree what you want the situation to turn out to be, a seal of divine authority comes upon it. After all, your power to decree originates from the Word of God.

As JOB 22:28-29 says, *"Thou shalt also decree a thing, and it shall be established unto thee: and the light shall shine upon thy ways. When men are cast down, then thou shalt say, There is lifting up; and he shall save the humble person."*

When you operate by decree, you are to operate in the opposite to the prevailing situation. Where there has been casting down, you are to decree lifting up. Where there has been defeat, you are to decree victory. Where there has been sickness, you are to decree health. Do this repeatedly, until your joy is full.

5. Add work to faith

Work creates an avenue for your faith to go into action. For example, if you are trusting God to give you a job, you will need to start making applications to suitable organisations that can employ you.

Faith needs corresponding actions to make it to work. In JAMES 2:26 we read: *"For as the body without the spirit is dead, so faith without works is dead also."*

If you have faith that God is able to help you pass an examination, then start reading, study and do thorough preparation for the examination. This effort of faith opens the door for God to start directing you to get the right result.

God directs the steps of a good man, as it says in PSALM 37:23: *"The steps of a good man are ordered by the LORD: and he delighteth in his way."* But if a good man makes no steps, how can God direct them? Until you start taking action, there will be nothing for your faith to work on.

6. Be bold

You must add boldness to your faith. You must not entertain fear when you are exercising your authority over situations of life, because fear is the opposite of faith.

As Jesus said in MATTHEW 8:26, *"Why are ye fearful, O ye of little faith? Then he arose, and rebuked the winds and the sea; and there was a great calm."*

Fear removes boldness and weakens faith. Boldness removes hesitation and enables you to exhibit singleness of mind as you face a situation. Boldness promotes courage – a vital attribute needed to face danger without fear.

7. Be stable

Faith will not work if you are unstable in your beliefs. Repetition of your statement of faith is an act of faith. Continue to act in faith until you see the result. Continually make your good confession based on the Word of God, aligning your actions and thoughts with your faith. For your faith to work there must be continual application of the principles of faith to your situations until your joy is full.

ROMANS 4:20 says that Abraham *"staggered not at the promise of God through unbelief; but was strong in faith, giving glory to God."*

"Staggered not" means Abraham was stable in his faith. There was no wavering in him. He was resolute.

> *"Watch ye, stand fast in the faith, quit you like men, be strong."*
> 1 CORINTHIANS 16:13.

Be firm in faith. Do not stop doing the right things of faith. Avoid alternative plans. Stick to a plan and keep working on it. If you want your faith to work for you, you will need to stick to the plan and keep on applying your faith to it.

In DANIEL 3, the king ordered the furnace to be heated seven times hotter than normal, to threaten the three Hebrews (Shadrach, Meshach and Abednego). But the three men of God remained unmovable. They stayed constant, never changing their confession. To make your faith work, you can't be changing your mind every time the situation takes a negative turn. Faith that will produce results does not give ground to the enemy.

When Israel was about to enter the Promised Land, God told the people not to be daunted by the number of their enemies: *"When thou goest out to battle against thine enemies, and seest horses, and chariots, and a people more than thou, be not afraid of them: for the*

LORD *thy God is with thee, which brought thee up out of the land of Egypt"* (DEUTERONOMY 20:1).

The kind of faith that produces results does not change its position because of unfavourable situations. Even when the resources seem to be going down, you must be stable in your faith.

> *"Now the just shall live by faith: but if any man draw back, my soul shall have no pleasure in him."* HEBREWS 10:38

Faith that brings results never gives up and turns back.

The peace of God helps keep our stability. Seek the peace that only He gives. His peace will keep your soul, spirit and body together and is good for your faith.

8. Be guided

To release your faith into action, you need to allow your faith to guide you in all your decisions regarding your situation. Do not act based on what you can see but what God can do.

> *"For we walk by faith, not by sight."* 2 CORINTHIANS 5:7

To walk by faith implies making decisions based on what you believe and not what you see. Physically, a situation may look ugly, but your decision should not be based on circumstances but on what you believe God is able to do concerning your situation.

9. Work by love

Acts of love set your faith in motion.

> *"For in Jesus Christ neither circumcision availeth any thing, nor uncircumcision; but faith which worketh by love."* GALATIANS 5:6.

Faith works through love. Your faith in God must influence you to be like God, and God is love.

One of the acts of love God shows us is giving: *"For God so loved the world, that he gave his only begotten Son, that whosoever believeth in him should not perish, but have everlasting life"* (JOHN 3:16).

Emulate God by being a giver. Giving opens the door to the supernatural. Demonstrate your love of God by being a giver to people around you, irrespective of who they are. It is possible to give and trust God for His specific intervention over certain situations of your life. Through hospitality, Abraham entertained angels and this led to the removal of barrenness in his life (GENESIS 18:1-3).

10. Put on joy

Joy makes your appearance attractive because it shows on your face. And a joyful attitude makes you an attractive person to the outside world. Joy also attracts the operation of the Holy Spirit. NEHEMIAH 8:10 says that *"the joy of the Lord is your strength"*. You need to exhibit joy and promote any activities that will bring more joy to your heart. A sorrowful heart does not create a conducive environment for the Holy Spirit to work through you, though He will comfort you if you seek Him in prayer.

The kingdom of God is about joy:

> *"For the kingdom of God is not meat and drink; but righteousness, and peace, and joy in the Holy Ghost."* ROMANS 14:17

And it is linked with faith:

> *"Although the fig tree shall not blossom, neither shall fruit be in the vines; the labour of the olive shall fail, and the fields shall yield no meat; the flock shall be cut off from the fold, and there shall be no herd in the stalls: Yet I will rejoice in the LORD, I will joy in the God of my salvation".* HABAKKUK 3:17-18

Habakkuk said he would keep on rejoicing despite the negative situation around him. Joy is a breeding ground for miracles. It creates an atmosphere where the Holy Spirit can operate.

That is why it is important for you to praise and worship God regularly. Be a worshipper. This will set your faith into motion.

Enemies of Faith

CHAPTER 7

"Submit yourselves therefore to God. Resist the devil, and he will flee from you"

JAMES 4:7

Enemies of faith are those factors that can be a hindrance to your trust in God.

Some believers start with faith in God but soon they change their position. It is very unlikely that you will intentionally decide to stop exercising faith in God; it usually happens in subtle ways. Therefore it is important for you to understand the factors that can come against your faith.

1. The devil

Satan hates believers of God and he will do everything possible to attack their faith in God. Even when you choose to exercise your authority over situations of life as a believer, the devil will cleverly arrange things to oppose your faith.

One of the ways the devil attacks your faith is by putting lies in your mind, in order to attack and defeat your faith. He can bombard your mind with a series of questions and promptings that are untrue.

The devil is the author of doubt. So whenever you begin to doubt God in your situation, be aware that the devil is at work.

JOHN 8:44 says: *"Ye are of your father the devil, and the lusts of your father ye will do. He was a murderer from the beginning, and abode not in the truth, because there is no truth in him. When he speaketh a lie, he speaketh of his own: for he is a liar, and the father of it."*

Satan is a liar. He lies to the believer to attack their faith in God. He questions their confidence. He makes them rationalise spiritual matters so as to lure them into human reasoning. If believers allow Satan to drag them into human thinking and wisdom, then their faith will gradually weaken until it vanishes away.

In ACTS 5:3, Ananias and Sapphira were deceived by the devil, which had serious consequences: *"But Peter said, Ananias, why hath Satan filled thine heart to lie to the Holy Ghost, and to keep back part of the price of the land?"*

Ananias and Sapphira had agreed by faith to sell something and bring the proceeds to God. When it was time for them to fulfil their pledge, Satan filled their hearts with lies. They embraced the lie and their faith eroded away.

When you suddenly start doubting God, Satan is at work. When you begin to hear messages and advice that are contrary to your faith, Satan is at work. When you feel like seeking a different way to get what you have been trusting God for, Satan is at work. When you see yourself thinking and acting contrary to faith, you must realise that Satan is at work. He is the enemy of your faith.

So how do we defeat the devil? By resisting him: *"Submit yourselves therefore to God. Resist the devil, and he will flee from you"* (JAMES 4:7).

Don't give in to his influence! You must not agree to any thought or prompting that makes you start doubting God. Refuse to think or speak or act in doubt. Do not tolerate questioning or entertain the possibility of doubting God. Do not reason with the devil. Evict him.

2. *The world*

'The world' in this context means the human system around you – the influence of society upon you, whether through politics, economics, cultural beliefs and moral standards, educational institutions or ideologies. The world is shaped by man making his own laws and forming his own opinions that are contrary to the Christian faith. Faith is supernatural – it operates on a totally different set of principles called the law of the spirit and life. The natural laws and all their ideas are opposite to the supernatural law on which faith operates. That is why it will be impossible for you to build your faith in God on worldly structures and its institutions, because they oppose God and each other. It is also important for you to know that some worldly systems are founded and managed by demonic forces. All these are enemies of faith in God.

The devil told Jesus that he was in charge of the world: *"And the devil, taking him up into an high mountain, shewed unto him all the kingdoms of the world in a moment of time. And the devil said unto him, All this power will I give thee, and the glory of them: for that is delivered unto me; and to whomsoever I will I give it"* (LUKE 4:5-6).

World systems are built on demonic influence and principles. That is why the world is filled with greed and every sort of wickedness.

> *"Love not the world, neither the things that are in the world. If any man love the world, the love of the Father is not in him. For all that is in the world, the lust of the flesh, and the lust of the eyes, and the pride of life, is not of the Father, but is of the world."* 1 JOHN 2:15-16

Every human institution outside of the Church operates in a way that is contrary to faith in God. That doesn't mean that there can't be good within institutions and people, but ultimately they are deceived by the devil and so lead you away from God's ways. There are only two kingdoms in the world – the kingdom of darkness and the kingdom of light.

Therefore it is wrong for you to identify what is possible and impossible according to the definitions and descriptions of the world systems. If you want to operate in faith in God, you must learn how to ignore the viewpoint of the world when it is contrary to God's will and purposes. If you want to build your faith, focus on the supernatural world and not the natural world, and believe that what God says is right – not what you hear from the world.

3. People

People who don't know Jesus are blinded to the truth by the enemy. They can't understand the things of God and the ways of faith.

1 CORINTHIANS 2:14 says: *"But the natural man receiveth not the things of the Spirit of God: for they are foolishness unto him: neither can he know them, because they are spiritually discerned."*

The natural man follows the desires of the flesh, and his thinking is guided by natural laws not spiritual laws. Such a man is unenlightened by the Holy Spirit and so he can't receive the things of the Spirit of God nor appreciate or understand them. He considers the demonstration of your faith as foolishness.

It's therefore not surprising that Christians are mocked for their faith. People who do this are called "scoffers" in 2 PETER 3:3, or "mockers" in some modern translations. They are enemies of your faith in God. Therefore, don't let the opinion of natural man influence your faith in God because he is blind towards faith. Don't listen to those who make fun of you – just pray for them.

4. Tradition

This is an inherited pattern of thought or action or beliefs or customs or culture, handed down from generation to generation.

It could become the principles that guide the way of life of people. It determines the way of bringing up children in that society, and many other aspects of life. People find it easy to follow tradition because they were born and raised in it. Tradition tends to influence the faith of people. Unfortunately, most of the traditions of men stand against biblical doctrines.

That is why you should be mindful of the culture you live in, because it may influence the way you think about God or the way you live out your faith.

Jesus made it clear that traditions, even religious traditions, can oppose God's Word: *"Making the word of God of none effect through your tradition, which ye have delivered: and many such like things do ye"* (MARK 7:13).

Tradition can become the enemy of faith in your life, if you exalt tradition above what the Word of God says concerning your situation. If there is a contradiction between the Word of God and your tradition, always choose to follow the Bible.

Do not use religious tradition to interpret the Bible or determine doctrine. If you want your faith to work you must not mix tradition with your faith in God. That is why you must constantly question the origin of your thoughts, beliefs or actions, to check if they are from your tradition or from the Word of God.

5. *The flesh*

This is another enemy of faith in God. If you want to walk in faith you have to learn how to put your flesh – your natural desires – under subjection. The carnal nature fights your spiritual nature, and that includes your emotions, if you allow them to determine how you react to situations. We need to be in control of our emotions.

The flesh hates pain, discomfort and inconveniences. You will need to master your flesh, control your temper and develop patience, so that your faith can be demonstrated in times of difficulty.

The flesh loves enjoyment, entertainment and pleasure. We need to ensure these things do not dominate our lives or contradict our faith. The flesh also loves food and drink, and can demand food when you want to fast for your spiritual empowerment.

When you feel like praying all night, the flesh may ask for sleep. You must also know that the flesh has 'voices' through which it can speak into your mind. Those voices can speak through what you hear, what you touch, what you taste or smell – all the senses can tempt us away from our faithfulness to the Lord and into sin.

The flesh also involves our mind. When you begin to entertain human reasoning and logic that contradicts your faith, then the flesh is at work. When negative imagination, sinful fantasies or fearful anxieties begin to flow into your mind and weaken your faith, the flesh is at work. When suddenly ideas drop into your mind that justify your sin or give you reasons not to pray, read your Bible, go to church or worship God, then your flesh is at work. You will need to arise and fight the flesh.

We are in a battle of flesh versus spirit: *"For the flesh lusteth against the Spirit, and the Spirit against the flesh: and these are contrary the one to the other: so that ye cannot do the things that ye would"* (GALATIANS 5:17).

Faith in God is spiritual and supernatural, while the flesh is carnal and natural. Flesh and faith don't work together. They are always in opposition. For this reason, Paul wrote: *"But I keep under my body, and bring it into subjection: lest that by any means, when I have preached to others, I myself should be a castaway"* (1 CORINTHIANS 9:27).

You will need to keep your flesh under subjection whenever it attempts to rise against your faith. Refuse to please the flesh when it makes its demands, especially when you are trusting God for certain miracles.

6. *Personal attributes*

These include intelligence, talent, knowledge and certain skills. If not well guided, personal attributes can bring temptations. They

Enemies of Faith

can make you begin to trust in yourself instead of God.

For example, those who have the skills of a trained soldier may be tempted to use them inappropriately, instead of trusting God for victory. If you are gifted in passing examinations, you may be tempted to put your trust in your own knowledge instead of God.

It can happen in a subtle way. You just do not see any reason why you should fail, based on your past achievements. So, you do not see any reason why you should exercise faith in God for giving you success; after all, you know how to deal with the situation yourself. This is a mistake.

God says in JEREMIAH 9:23: *"Let not the wise man glory in his wisdom, neither let the mighty man glory in his might, let not the rich man glory in his riches..."*

Your glory should be in your faith in God, not any personal attributes. This is because no matter how much you know in life, there is always something you do not know. Man, born of flesh, is full of limitations. Whatever your ability, never stop exercising faith in God.

7. *Fear*

This is another powerful enemy of faith. Fear is an unpleasant emotion created by the threat of danger. Usually, such danger is imaginary, not real. Fear breeds doubt and pessimism. Fear acts in opposition to faith.

When you allow fear, it takes away your ability to resist and overcome difficulties. It makes you anticipate failure instead of success. Fear exacerbates the problem and diminishes the possibility of a solution. It takes away boldness.

A believer who has fear will not be able to show courage in any challenging situation. Fear has already defeated him, so, he can't stand. If you want your faith to work, you have to defeat fear. Faith can't work without courage. Your faith can't succeed when you have already been captured by fear.

But why should we be afraid, when we have the Spirit who raised Christ from the dead within us?

> *"For ye have not received the spirit of bondage again to fear; but ye have received the Spirit of adoption, whereby we cry, Abba, Father."* ROMANS 8:15

Fear is a spirit of bondage because it takes away freedom. You are not yourself when you are under fear.

One of the ways to overcome fear is simply to resist it when it comes to you. Maintain your courage and rebuke the spirit that wants to make you afraid of the situation. Rebuke the spirit that is speaking into your mind that the situation will get worse or go badly. Fear is in the mind. Therefore, continually renewing your mind using the Word of God will counteract fear.

8. Ignorance

This is lack of knowledge about God and His principles of operation. Your faith can't be effective when you base it on wrong principles. The strength of your faith is dependent on the depth of your knowledge of God.

> *"And such as do wickedly against the covenant shall he corrupt by flatteries: but the people that do know their God shall be strong, and do exploits."* DANIEL 11:32

You need faith to do exploits and your faith needs knowledge of God to be effective. Therefore it's important that you increase your knowledge of God. For example, if you are trusting God for healing or you want to exercise your spiritual authority over sickness, it is important for you to know the promises of God about healing, so that your faith will be based on what you know to be true and not on assumptions. How correctly you apply your faith is determined by the level of knowledge of God that you have.

9. Idolatory

> *"Little children, keep yourselves from idols."* 1 JOHN 5:21

Idols are those things in your life that receive your worship – the worship that you are supposed to give to God. Those things in your life that you adore can become your idols. For example, it is good that you adore your wife, but if you put her before God then that is idolatry. Alternatively, it may be your job, if you put your career before serving God. Or it may be your possessions – if you can't give them up when God asks you to.

Such things control your heart. They are idols in your life. Your faith in God can't be effective when you give worship that is due to God to something else. Whatever takes the place of God in your life is your idol.

Keep yourself from idols. If not, they will drag you away from trusting God. Faith is a matter of the heart and if God does not take central position in your heart, your faith in God will not be effective. Idol worship is an enemy of faith in God.

10. A religious spirit

A spirit of religion is an enemy of faith. One thing this spirit does is to make you stick to the old and reject the new. Even when you are convinced about the new, you would rather join the new and old together instead of letting the old go. This hinders faith in God.

Jesus said: *"No man putteth a piece of new cloth unto an old garment, for that which is put in to fill it up taketh from the garment, and the rent is made worse. Neither do men put new wine into old bottles: else the bottles break, and the wine runneth out, and the bottles perish: but they put new wine into new bottles, and both are preserved"* (MATTHEW 9:16-17).

The old and the new can't go together. The old will inhibit the new. More than that, the spirit of religion will prevent you from seeing the value of the new things God is doing, especially in your own life. For example, your faith will not work if you apply it to open a door that God has closed in your life. The religious spirit will influence you to stick with the old that God has abandoned because He is finished with it. He wants to do new things. Do not trust God to open the door He has closed, rather, trust Him to open new and greater doors of opportunity for you.

You will be practising blind faith if you keep on putting your faith in things that God has declared are past in your life. Instead, trust God for new things. Get rid of the religious spirit that is hindering you from seeing the new things of God.

11. Identity

This is the way you see yourself. The way you see yourself will affect your faith in God.

For example, if you see yourself as nobody, it will affect how you exercise faith over the issues of your life. If you see yourself as somebody with no spiritual influence, then your faith can't work for you because your view of who you are has already defeated you.

Gideon saw himself as insignificant when the angel of the Lord appeared to him and said: *"The LORD is with thee, thou mighty man of valour"* (JUDGES 6:12).

God looked at Gideon and saw a mighty man of valour, because He knew what Gideon would become. He saw the potential. But Gideon didn't: *"And the LORD looked upon him, and said, Go in this thy might, and thou shalt save Israel from the hand of the Midianites:*

have not I sent thee? And he said unto him, Oh my Lord, wherewith shall I save Israel? behold, my family is poor in Manasseh, and I am the least in my father's house" (JUDGES 6:14-15).

God saw Gideon as a channel of deliverance that was capable of delivering Israel. But unfortunately Gideon saw himself as nobody – a person with low social status. He had low self-esteem. He saw himself as a man with no potential. Even when Gideon eventually agreed to go into battle for Israel, his view about himself had a negative effect on his faith.

When you do not believe in yourself, you can't believe in your faith in God. For your faith in God to work, you will need to see yourself as God sees you. To God, you are a king *("I have said, Ye are gods; and all of you are children of the most High"* – PSALM 82:6). If you see yourself as a king then you will believe that when you issue a command to a situation, it will be done. Kings rule by decree.

12. *Unforgiveness*

This is an act of holding onto an offence you suffered from somebody. This will hinder your spiritual effectiveness; it will not let your faith work.

Unforgiveness is an act of hatred towards the person who offends you. But faith in God works by love. A heart filled with bitterness and hatred towards a fellow human being can't decree something in faith and expect it to happen. Faith in God works by love: *"For in Jesus Christ neither circumcision availeth any thing, nor uncircumcision; but faith which worketh by love"* (GALATIANS 5:6).

You can't exercise faith in God with bitterness in your heart. As Jesus said: *"Therefore if thou bring thy gift to the altar, and there rememberest that thy brother hath ought against thee; leave there thy gift before the altar, and go thy way; first be reconciled to thy brother, and then come and offer thy gift"* (MATTHEW 5:23-24).

In this teaching, if a person brought an offering to the altar (which was an act of faith) but remembered that there was an offence to be sorted out between himself and someone else, he should make peace with that other person first, otherwise his act of faith would not be rewarded. The supernatural does not obey the word of an unforgiving person.

13. Pride

A proud man has a high opinion of himself. He sees himself the way he is not. A proud man considers himself better than other people.

Faith requires humility for it to work effectively. Humility is the nature of Jesus: *"Let this mind be in you, which was also in Christ Jesus: who, being in the form of God, thought it not robbery to be equal with God: but made himself of no reputation, and took upon him the form of a servant, and was made in the likeness of men…"* (PHILIPPIANS 2:5-7).

Jesus is a person of humility. He is not proud and does not think highly about himself, despite being the Son of God. If your faith in God is going to produce results, you will need to have the mind of Jesus Christ – a mind of humility. As Peter said: *"Likewise, ye younger, submit yourselves unto the elder. Yea, all of you be subject one to another, and be clothed with humility: for God resisteth the proud, and giveth grace to the humble"* (1 PETER 5:5).

One of the blessings of humility is divine grace. You will need divine grace for your faith to work. Pride will rob you of this grace. Pride puts God against you instead of being on your side. God will not let the prayer of a proud man succeed. Avoid pride so that your faith can be effective.

14. Sin

> *"Whosoever committeth sin transgresseth also the law: for sin is the transgression of the law."* 1 JOHN 3:4

Enemies of Faith

Every act of unrighteousness is a sin. Whoever practises sin is considered a law breaker by God. God does not relate to law breakers. Sin is an enemy of faith in God. It destroys your spiritual sensitivity. It weakens your faith.

Sin makes you ineffective in the realm of the supernatural. With sin in your life you can't control the supernatural. The devil is the author of sin and whoever sins is under his bondage. You can't be practising sin and expect Satan to obey your commands.

Sin separates you from God. Even the prayer of a sinner is an abomination to God, unless it is a prayer of repentance and seeking forgiveness. To make your faith effective, depart from sin. Ask God's forgiveness. He is able to forgive all sin:

> *"And you, being dead in your sins and the uncircumcision of your flesh, hath he quickened together with him, having forgiven you all trespasses."* COLOSSIANS 2:13

Making the Word Work for You

CHAPTER 8

"For unto us was the gospel preached, as well as unto them: but the word preached did not profit them, not being mixed with faith in them that heard it."

HEBREWS 4:2

The Word of God can only profit you when you mix it with faith. When the Word of God is believed, it produces the results that God promises in it. You can make the Word of God work for you. That may sound selfish but it's not, because God loves you and wants the best for you. He has given us promises in His Word for a reason – so that they may be fulfilled and we can be blessed

In this chapter we shall consider a case study from the Bible to teach you how to mix the Word of God with faith to get the results that God wants for you.

"And it came to pass after many days, that the word of the LORD came to Elijah in the third year, saying, Go, shew thyself unto Ahab; and I will send rain upon the earth." 1 KINGS 18:1

In this verse, the word of God came to Elijah the prophet. God told Elijah that He would send rain. This promise came after over three years of drought in the land. The man of God believed the word he received and started acting on it.

Similarly, a word from God can come to you through studying the Word of God – the Bible. The Spirit of God can draw your attention to certain promises in the Bible that address your present situation. Irrespective of the seriousness of your present challenge, you must believe that word.

> *"And Elijah said unto Ahab, Get thee up, eat and drink; for there is a sound of abundance of rain. So Ahab went up to eat and to drink. And Elijah went up to the top of Carmel; and he cast himself down upon the earth, and put his face between his knees, and said to his servant, Go up now, look toward the sea. And he went up, and looked, and said, There is nothing. And he said, Go again seven times. And it came to pass at the seventh time, that he said, Behold, there ariseth a little cloud out of the sea, like a man's hand. And he said, Go up, say unto Ahab, Prepare thy chariot, and get thee down, that the rain stop thee not. And it came to pass in the mean while, that the heaven was black with clouds and wind, and there was a great rain. And Ahab rode, and went to Jezreel. And the hand of the LORD was on Elijah; and he girded up his loins, and ran before Ahab to the entrance of Jezreel."* 1 KINGS 18:41-46

This story shows how Elijah made the word he received from the Lord in verse 1 work. The word came to pass as he received it from the Lord. Elijah mixed the word with faith. This is evident from the actions he took:

1. *He visualised the word*

> *"And Elijah said unto Ahab, Get thee up, eat and drink; for there is a sound of abundance of rain."* 1 KINGS 18:4

To visualise implies forming a mental picture of something that is invisible. Elijah didn't say that there "will be" an abundance of rain; he said that "there is" an abundance of rain – that was said in faith. But he probably also thought that it had been a long time since it last rained, so if it rained now it would be very heavy.

Whenever you receive a word from God, the first thing to do is to form a mental picture of it. Turn that word into a picture in your imagination. This turns the word into a reality in your spirit. The word will no longer appear strange and abstract to you, but a picture of an existing image.

> *"These all died in faith, not having received the promises, but having seen them afar off, and were persuaded of them, and embraced them, and confessed that they were strangers and pilgrims on the earth."*
> HEBREWS 11:13

The heroes and heroines of faith saw the promises of God "afar off". That is, they developed a telescopic vision of God's promises – they saw what was coming from God, by faith, and trusted Him to keep His Word. At this stage, the word they received started appearing real in their imagination. A similar thing happened to Abraham in GENESIS 15:5: *"And he brought him forth abroad, and said, Look now toward heaven, and tell the stars, if thou be able to number them: and he said unto him, So shall thy seed be."*

God helped Abraham to develop a mental picture of his plan for him, by comparing the number of Abraham's descendants with the number of stars in the sky. This enabled him to see what would happen in the future when the promise was fulfilled.

For example, maybe you are a couple who have not yet had the child you wish for. God has sent you His word. As it is written in EXODUS 23:26: *"There shall nothing cast their young, nor be barren, in thy land:*

the number of thy days I will fulfil." This is a promise of God to you as believers, that you shall not die barren. You can form a mental picture of this word by imagining how your home will look with many children around you.

The advantage of having a mental picture of what God is going to do in your life is to help you to see yourself in the light of future, not the present. The devil wants you to evaluate your entire life based on your present situation that is passing away, but you must refuse this. Evaluate your life based on the glorious life awaiting you tomorrow. Develop a sanctified imagination and start imagining your life according to the word you have received from God, not your current circumstances.

2. He actualised the word

Elijah actualised the word he received from God. This means to include it in your plans and decisions – to act on it.

> *"And it came to pass at the seventh time, that he said, Behold, there ariseth a little cloud out of the sea, like a man's hand. And he said, Go up, say unto Ahab, Prepare thy chariot, and get thee down that the rain stop thee not."* 1 KINGS 18:44

Elijah told King Ahab to move fast because the rain is coming. That is, he told the king to consider the rain in his journey. Elijah included the word he received from God in his counsel, advice and decision.

When you receive a word from God, start including it in your decision-making from that time onwards. For example, if God has told you that you will buy a car next year, then start learning to drive if you can't drive already, and get a licence, so that you will be ready – but also so that your actions are aligned with your faith. Also, start including a car of your own in your plans for the future. This all shows God that you really do believe him.

Whatever word you receive from God, start making plans in the light of the word you received.

> *"(As it is written, I have made thee a father of many nations,) before him whom he believed, even God, who quickeneth the dead, and calleth those things which be not as though they were."* ROMANS 4:17

Start calling things which are not as if they were.

For example, you may be sick and God has sent you this word from 1PETER 2:24: *"Who his own self bare our sins in his own body on the tree, that we, being dead to sins, should live unto righteousness: by whose stripes ye were healed."* If so, from the time you receive this word, start regarding yourself as an able person with sound health. Begin to actualise the word.

3. *He embraced the word*

To embrace something means to admire or to fall in love with something, and to be passionate about it.

Elijah loved what God told him – that God would send the rain. This is evident from the passion he showed towards this word. He kept on sending his servant to look at the sky for rain. He did not let his servant rest until it rained. He did not let himself rest until it rained.

When God gives you a promise, embrace it, as evidence that you really desire its manifestation in your life. Embracing it helps you to absorb the word into your life. The word becomes part of you.

> *"These all died in faith, not having received the promises, but having seen them afar off, and were persuaded of them, and embraced them, and confessed that they were strangers and pilgrims on the earth."* HEBREWS 11:13

The people of faith embraced what God showed them He would do. That is, they allowed God's promise to capture their minds and hearts.

This is important, because whatever captures your mind will control your thoughts. Whatever controls your thoughts will control your speech and actions, and this will control your destiny. To embrace God's promise is an indication that you really want it. This is very significant, because if your attitude and actions signify that you don't really want the promises of God, then they will not be given to you. That is why you must not fault God's provision, otherwise you may lose it.

So, when God promises you something, embrace it, otherwise it will not come to pass. When God shows you a picture of your tomorrow, love the thought of it. If you love the promise you receive from God, you set the right conditions for it to gradually unfold in your life.

4. He spoke the word out

Elijah confessed the word he received from God. Elijah said the rain was coming. He verbalised it. He said it just as God had said it to him. Elijah agreed with the word of God about the situation. It is important that you speak to your situation with the word God has given you about your situation, not your own word or the word of the enemy.

Here are three points on the importance of confession:

A. It draws the power of God into your that situation to work out the word. ECCLESIASTES 8:4 SAYS: *"Where the word of a king is, there is power: and who may say unto him, What doest thou?"* Whenever you confess the word of God repeatedly into your situation, you will be drawing the power of God into action on that situation. That is, you activate the power of God by the word God gave you – because His word is powerful and active.

B. You signal to God how He should handle your case. God will deal with you according to your own word – that is, according to what He hears you saying. NUMBERS 14:28 says: *"Say unto them, As* *truly as I live, saith the Lord, as ye have spoken in mine ears, so will I do to you..."* God respects your free will; He will respect what you say.

C. It prevents the devil from putting his own word in your mouth. If you keep on speaking the word God has given you, you will not give the devil a chance of putting his own words in your mouth. This keeps the devil off your case, because he accesses your life to do his evil work when you use negative words.

5. He acted on the word

Elijah acted on the word he received from God. The word moved him into action. This is evident from the fact that he asked his servant to check the sky for rain several times, while also praying hard for the rain to come.

Whenever you receive a word from God, you must identify your part in the word you received. That is, what is it that you need to do to complement what God will do concerning the promise?

If you don't know what you need to do concerning the word you received from God, ask God to help you to identify your responsibility. You must know the action you need to take that aligns with the word you received. There is always something you have to do, whenever God sends you His word, because *"faith, if it hath not works, is dead, being alone"* (JAMES 2:17).

This implies that faith alone can't produce a result. It needs some ingredients such as work (action/step of faith). Action is needed in order to make faith work. The faith that produces results is operational faith.

For example, if God has told you that He will build you a house, then start working on the plan and plan how you want the house to be. Start working it out now. Take a step of faith.

6. He stood on the word

Elijah rejected the bad report of his servant six times. As the servant came to tell him there was no rain, he kept on sending him back. Elijah stood on the word he had received.

Irrespective of the negative situation around you, you must not move away from what God has told you. You must resist the devil and reject every contrary opinion of men. If you want the words of God to work for you, don't negotiate or surrender to the contradictory situation.

You must stand on the word you receive: *"Moreover, brethren, I declare unto you the gospel which I preached unto you, which also ye have received, and wherein ye stand..."* (1 CORINTHIANS 15:1).

For example, if you received the word of God of 1 PETER 2:24 (*"by whose stripes ye were healed"*) concerning your sickness, but you still feel pain after it, you have to stand on this word, and continue to confess it until that sickness disappears.

7. He expected the fulfilment of the word

Elijah was expecting the rain to fall just as God said. He was continually on the look-out for the rain. Similarly, you also must be on the look-out for the fulfilment of what God has told you.

How should you expect it?

Expect the fulfilment of the word God sent to you concerning your situation anytime, unless God has told you the precise time and location.

1 THESSALONIANS 5:2 indicates that the fulfilment of the Word of God could be sudden, without warning: *"For yourselves know perfectly that the day of the lord so cometh as a thief in the night."* Therefore, you must be alert, vigilant and awake. Constantly be on the look-out for your miracle.

8. He prayed the word into existence

Elijah prayed the word he received from God into existence. He continued to pray until the promise of God was established.

But the question is: why did Elijah need to pray so intensely like that, after all, whatever God promises will come to pass? God had promised the rain so it was going to rain whether Elijah prayed or not. But whenever God sends you a word, it implies that you have a responsibility for making it to come to pass. God chooses to involve us in the fulfilment of His promises.

> *"And it came to pass after many days, that the word of the Lord came to Elijah in the third year, saying, Go, shew thyself unto Ahab; and I will send rain upon the earth."* 1 KINGS 18:1

It's clear from this verse that God had promised to send the rain but He did not state the timing. Instead, God was trusting Elijah to determine the timing.

As soon as God promised to send the rain, the rain came into existence in the spiritual realm, but it is important to realise that the rain would remain in the spiritual realm until the power of Elijah's prayer drew it into physical existence. Perhaps, if Elijah had not prayed, it would still have rained because God had said it would, but it may not have happened until many days or even years later.

There are many fulfilments of God's promises that are being delayed today because people don't know that they determine the timing through their prayers. There are certain promises of God that will not come to pass early in your life until you pray intensely concerning them.

There are many people who have received a word from God, but because they don't understand that they need to pray it into existence they are yet to witness the manifestation of it. Pray until the promise of God comes into existence in your situation.

The Voice of Dominion

———————————————————————— CHAPTER 9

> *"And God said, Let us make man in our image, after our likeness: and let them have dominion over the fish of the sea, and over the fowl of the air, and over the cattle, and over all the earth, and over every creeping thing that creepeth upon the earth."*
>
> GENESIS 1:26

In the beginning, God gave mankind dominion over the earth. Satan now has dominion over the world, but not where the Church opposes him. God wants us to rule over what happens on the earth.

EPHESIANS 1:20-23 says: *"Which he wrought in Christ, when he raised him from the dead, and set him at his own right hand in the heavenly places, far above all principality, and power, and might, and dominion, and every name that is named, not only in this world, but also in that which is to come: and hath put all things under his feet, and gave him to be the head over all things to the church, which is his body, the fulness of him that filleth all in all."*

The above verse shows that Jesus has dominion over the devil and all things, and ROMANS 8:17 says that we are *"heirs of God and co-heirs with Christ, if indeed we share in his sufferings in order that we may also share in his glory."*

So if we are co-heirs, we have inherited the same power over the devil and Christ's authority over all things. This enables believers to exercise control over the situations of their lives.

The earth and all other creatures understand the fact that believers have dominion. But unfortunately, the devil and all his cohorts will appear as if they are ignorant of your dominion as a believer. It is therefore necessary that you speak and instruct the situations of your life with a voice of authority. The way you speak matters, as it will determine how the situations will respond to your word of instruction.

When you speak the word of God to your situation, you must speak as Jesus spoke to situations when He was physically here on earth. Jesus used His life to show us how to speak with a voice of dominion over the situations of our lives.

1. Jesus speaks of His heavenly identities

If you are to exercise faith over the situations of life, you must make your identity known to the spiritual realm. In the realm of the spirit, who is talking matters, for the forces of the supernatural are a hierarchy of principalities and powers. They only respond to the authority they know is above them, so they will ask for the identity of the person.

It is not every believer that can command the supernatural. This is because some believers are not sure of their heavenly identities, so they have no confidence that they can control the unseen forces through their faith.

Because identity matters in the realm of the spirit, Jesus spoke about His heavenly identities in many situations, to teach us that we should let the creation know that we know who we are in Christ.

In JOHN 6:35, Jesus said: *"I am the bread of life: he that cometh to me shall never hunger; and he that believeth on me shall never thirst."*

Jesus spoke of himself as the bread of life. Similarly, in John 10:7, Jesus spoke of Himself as the door. These identities come from heaven not from this earth, and this compels creation to respond to His command.

This implies that, as a believer, if you are going to exercise dominion over the situations of your life, you must learn how to speak your heavenly identities to those situations. Let the force and power behind the situation know who is talking, and that you know who you are in Christ.

For example, one of your heavenly identities is stated in Isaiah 35:10: *"And the ransomed of the Lord shall return, and come to Zion with songs and everlasting joy upon their heads: they shall obtain joy and gladness, and sorrow and sighing shall flee away."*

You are the ransomed of the Lord. That is, the Lord has set you free from every kind of captivity. Therefore, no power or spirit has got any right to put you in any form of captivity anymore. The Lord has bought you with a price – the blood of Jesus.

Standing on this identity, you can speak to any bondage in your life that you have been bought by the Lord from captivity; it is therefore impossible for you to be brought into any form of captivity anymore. You can exercise your faith by taking authority over that bondage by commanding it to be broken in your life.

As a believer, it is written in PSALM 82:6 that *"ye are gods; and all of you are children of the most High."*

This implies that you are the representative of the almighty God. You carry the authority of God. Therefore, whatever you decree is decreed by God and whatever you command is commanded by God. This means that every creature is bound to obey your voice as if it is the voice of God, because the authority of God dwells in you.

When you are exercising faith over situations of your life, speak with the consciousness of your heavenly identities. Do not speak the word of God with the identities the world has given you, but speak using the identities that God has given you. This boosts the effectiveness of your faith over situations.

2. *Jesus speaks as the oracle of God*

Jesus exercised dominion because He spoke to the situations of life as the oracle of God. That is, He spoke the mind of God concerning every situation.

In JOHN 14:10, Jesus said, *"Believest thou not that I am in the Father, and the Father in me? The words that I speak unto you I speak not of myself: but the Father that dwelleth in me, he doeth the works."*

That is, Jesus mouth was the mouthpiece of God. This implies that whenever He opened His mouth to speak, it was God speaking through Him, not Himself.

Similarly, you also must speak as the oracle of God concerning your situation. You must speak about your circumstances with the mind of God. The mind of God is revealed in the Word of God. In general terms, this is summarised in JEREMIAH 29:11: *"For I know the thoughts that I think toward you, saith the Lord, thoughts of peace, and not of evil, to give you an expected end."*

This simple summary implies that God's promises for your life in all situations are good and positive. So as you face your difficulties and decisions, remember that God has promised only good things for you. He is on your side!

Therefore, as you exercise your faith, let this promise of God reflect in your voice as you speak to your situations. Speak good and positive outcomes to your situation, irrespective of the magnitude of the problem. Even when you don't know specifically what God has in mind concerning that problem or issue, just keep on speaking good and positive outcomes to it.

It is just a matter of time before God gives you *"an expected end"* (JEREMIAH 29:11), or as modern translations put it, "hope and a future." This will manifest in your life as the Word of God has promised in this verse.

As a believer, through your faith in God, you can exercise dominion over situations of life by standing on the promises of God.

3. Jesus speaks the end result

Bible confirms that whenever Jesus confronted a situation, He spoke the outcome He desired. He always spoke results.

For example, in MATTHEW 8:3, Jesus *"put forth his hand, and touched him, saying, I will; be thou clean. And immediately his leprosy was cleansed."*

In this story, Jesus spoke the outcome – to be clean.

Similarly, faith will require that you speak the outcome you desire to your situation. This is a way of exercising dominion over things in life that are not conforming to God's "good, and acceptable, and perfect, will' for you (ROMANS 12:2).

You should stop speaking about the problem to your problem and start speaking the solution to your problem. For example, don't speak about fear to things that make you afraid, but speak liberty concerning your fear. Speak defeat over your battle. Speak healing to your sickness. Speak your desire to your situation. By doing this, you will be enforcing your desire – and God's will – upon the situation.

For example, when David faced Goliath in 1 SAMUEL 17:46, he told the giant: *"This day will the Lord deliver thee into mine hand; and I will smite thee, and take thine head from thee; and I will give the carcases of the host of the Philistines this day unto the fowls of the air, and to the wild beasts of the earth; that all the earth may know that there is a God in Israel."*

David spoke the outcome he desired concerning Goliath and it came true. David did not speak about the height and the strength of Goliath, but the outcome of the battle. He spoke defeat to the enemy. He told his battle that he would be victorious over it, and so be it. As you exercise your faith, speak your expectations to that situation. By doing so, you will be directly exercising dominion over that situation, which will force it to end with your desire.

4. Jesus speaks judgementally

In our society, we are often told that we shouldn't be judgemental. And indeed we should not condemn other people. But there are times when we need to be judgemental – not about people but over situations.

Jesus operated as a judge over the situations He faced and He pronounced judgement against them. He determined the fate of His attackers by His own word. For example, MATTHEW 21:19 says that when Jesus *"saw a fig tree in the way, he came to it, and found nothing thereon, but leaves only, and said unto it, Let no fruit grow on thee henceforward for ever. And presently the fig tree withered away."*

Jesus pronounced judgement against the unfruitful fig tree. In some other situations, Jesus cast demons into the sea and desert. He judged them.

Similarly, as a believer, you have power to pronounce judgement against your enemy (the devil). By faith, you can pronounce judgement against the forces of darkness behind your problems. The judgement gives clarity on what you want the end of your enemy to be. Learn how to pronounce judgement against your enemy. Determine the outcome of your situation by your word.

Because God has given you dominion, it is your responsibility to determine the end of your enemy. By faith you can pronounce judgement against the forces that are making your life miserable. By faith you can pronounce judgement against the forces holding you captive.

5. Jesus speaks setting the boundary

In MARK 9:25, *"When Jesus saw that the people came running together, he rebuked the foul spirit, saying unto him, Thou dumb and deaf spirit, I charge thee, come out of him, and enter no more into him."*

Jesus commanded the demons to come out of the man, with an instruction never to come back into this man's life again. Jesus set the boundary for the future activities of those demons. Those demons did not die, they would still be alive and operating, but they would never come to that man again. They might go to another person's life, but not that man's.

As a believer, the dominion God gives you allows you to set the boundary for the enemy as regards your life. You can limit the future activities of the enemy concerning your life by what you say.

For example, NAHUM 1:9 indicates that God does not want you to suffer twice: *"What do ye imagine against the Lord? he will make an utter end: affliction shall not rise up the second time."*

This word of God empowers you as a believer to set the boundary for the enemy activities concerning your life. Don't just command the spirit of sickness to come out of your life, tell that spirit to never come near your life again. By faith, you can instruct certain problems to come out of your life and never return anymore. By faith, you can command that problem never to return to your bloodline anymore. By faith, as you pronounce judgement on a sickness troubling your life, you can also instruct that sickness to never return to your life or that of your family. By setting such boundaries, you will make your life a no-go area for the future activities of the terrible spirit that is causing your problem.

6. Jesus speaks aloud

For your faith to be effective, it will require exercising dominion over the situations of life by speaking aloud.

Whenever Jesus wanted His will to be done in situations, He always spoke aloud. For example: "And when he thus had spoken, he cried with a loud voice, Lazarus, come forth" (JOHN 11:43).

In this story of the resurrection of Lazarus, Jesus was dealing with the spirit of death, so He spoke aloud. Also, when Jesus was dealing with the storm in MARK 4:39, He spoke aloud.

In REVELATION 1:15, Jesus' voice is so loud that it sounds like "many waters" – the rushing waters of a mighty river or flood.

For your faith to be effective, it is imperative that you speak out the word of God you are standing on to overcome your situation. You need to verbalise it. This is because the demonic spirits that usually promote the problems of life will only respond to what they hear you saying.

They can't read your mind, neither can they read your heart or imagination. You will need to speak aloud so that any demonic spirit involved can obey what they hear. You can't command demons and principalities by talking to them in your mind; you have to speak out aloud.

7. Jesus speaks authoritatively

> *"For he taught them as one having authority, and not as the scribes."*
> MATTHEW 7:29

Jesus speaks with authority. Faith speaks with authority. To exercise dominion, you need to speak to situations in your life with authority.

Declare the Word of God over your situation with the authority God has vested in you as His child.

How do you speak with authority?

A. Speak in your own right. That is, you speak without taking instruction from anybody. For example, in JOHN 5:27 Jesus says that God had *"given him [Jesus] authority to execute judgment also, because he is the son of man"*.

This clarifies that Jesus did not need to take any further permission from God to act, because God has already given him the authority to act independently. Jesus has the fullness of God.

Similarly, as a Christian, you also have the fullness of God residing inside of you, so you can speak in your own right to your situations of your life. You can speak your desire to your situation. Declare your expectation to your situation. You have the Spirit of God within you, so every word from your mouth has the touch of the Spirit of God.

B. Speak with a commanding tone. Don't be shy or timid. When Jesus raised Lazarus from the dead, *"he cried with a loud voice, Lazarus, come forth"* (JOHN 11:43). As a believer you must know that you have dominion over created things. Therefore you must speak to a situation in the same commanding way as Jesus. A command exercises control over the situation – irrespective of whether it is a matter of life and death.

Do not speak to problem as if you are begging it, but speak with a command. As a believer, do not ask sickness to depart from your life, because if demons are behind it, they have no pity. The only word they understand is a command.

C. Speak with confidence. This means speaking with the voice of assurance, not in fear, shyness or timidity.

Jesus spoke in the knowledge that God always hears him – not just some of the time but all of the time. He said: *"And I knew that thou hearest me always: but because of the people which stand by I said it, that they may believe that thou hast sent me"* (JOHN 11:42).

Jesus was not afraid of the situation. He never worried that Lazarus might not be raised. To exercise dominion, you will need to speak with confidence to the situations of life, without any sign of fear. A mind filled with fear will not speak with assurance even if it speaks the Word of God into a situation.

D. Speak one possibility. To speak with authority will require speaking only one possibility concerning the situation. There should be no alternative solution or route. No hesitation.

As soon as Jesus *"thus had spoken, he cried with a loud voice, Lazarus, come forth"* (JOHN 11:43). Jesus was specific about his expectation that the dead man would obey His word – there was no equivocation or back-up plan. His prayer indicates clear direction. There is no alternative result in mind.

When you speak with clear direction, your demand becomes non-negotiable. For the effective exercising of dominion, there should be no wavering, no hesitation, no doubt and just one solution on the table. By faith, stick to your expectation and soon, the situation will respond to your control.

E. Speak with irresistible power

> *"For I will give you a mouth and wisdom, which all your adversaries shall not be able to gainsay nor resist."* LUKE 21:15

In these words, Jesus promises that He will make the word of your mouth irresistible to your enemy. That is, your word will carry authority that can't be faulted.

The Voice of Dominion

As you exercise your faith over situations of life, it is important that you remember that your word carries power. If your word cannot move you, then it will not move the enemy or situation.

Using Your Faith to Defeat Hopeless Situations

CHAPTER 10

"we walk by faith not by sight"

2 Corinthians 5:7

Faith can be used to defeat a hopeless situation in life. People lose hope when a sick person eventually dies. People lose hope when a marriage filled with crisis eventually ends in divorce.

A hopeless situation is like death. Death is the end – there's no going back, no further chance of a solution. That's how a hopeless situation feels – there is nothing that can be done about it now.

Therefore, if you know how to release your faith to raise the dead, then, you can release your faith to solve any other hopeless situation of life! This chapter reveals how you can release your faith to defeat a hopeless situation, using death as the ultimate example of such a situation.

Faith can bring back to life a dead business, a marriage, someone's health, a vision, a dream, etc. If faith can defeat death then, it can defeat any problem of life that is hopeless in human eyes, irrespective of its magnitude or the power behind it.

Faith THAT ALWAYS WINS

HEBREWS 11:35 says that *"women received their dead raised to life again"*. These women of faith saw death overcome. Whether it was their dead relative, dead hope, dead blessings, dead career or any good thing that had died in their lives, it came back to life again. They released their faith to defeat their hopeless situations.

How can you release your faith to defeat your hopeless situation?

Look at the example of Elisha and the Shunammite woman:

And he said, About this season, according to the time of life, thou shalt embrace a son. And she said, Nay, my lord, thou man of God, do not lie unto thine handmaid. And the woman conceived, and bare a son at that season that Elisha had said unto her, according to the time of life. And when the child was grown, it fell on a day, that he went out to his father to the reapers. And he said unto his father, My head, my head. And he said to a lad, Carry him to his mother. And when he had taken him, and brought him to his mother, he sat on her knees till noon, and then died. And she went up, and laid him on the bed of the man of God, and shut the door upon him, and went out. And she called unto her husband, and said, Send me, I pray thee, one of the young men, and one of the asses, that I may run to the man of God, and come again. And he said, Wherefore wilt thou go to him to day? it is neither new moon, nor sabbath. And she said, It shall be well. Then she saddled an ass, and said to her servant, Drive, and go forward; slack not thy riding for me, except I bid thee.

So she went and came unto the man of God to mount Carmel. And it came to pass, when the man of God saw her afar off, that he said to Gehazi his servant, Behold, yonder is that Shunammite: Run now, I pray thee, to meet her, and say unto her, Is it well with thee? is it well with thy husband? is it well with the child? And she answered, It is well: And when she came to the man of God to the hill, she caught him by the feet: but Gehazi came near to thrust her away. And the man of God said, Let her alone; for her soul is vexed within her: and the Lord hath hid it from me, and hath not told me. Then she said, Did I desire a son of my lord? did I not say, Do not deceive me? Then he said to Gehazi, Gird up thy loins, and take my staff in thine hand, and go thy way: if thou meet any man, salute him not; and if any salute thee, answer him not again: and lay my staff upon the face of the child. And the mother of the child said, As the Lord liveth, and as thy soul liveth, I will not leave thee. And he arose, and followed her. And Gehazi passed on before them, and laid the staff upon the face of the child; but there was neither voice, nor hearing. Wherefore he went again to meet him, and told him, saying, The child is not awaked.

And when Elisha was come into the house, behold, the child was dead, and laid upon his bed. He went in therefore, and shut the door upon them twain, and prayed unto the Lord. And he went up, and lay upon the child, and put his mouth upon his mouth, and his eyes upon his eyes, and his hands upon his hands: and stretched himself upon the child; and the flesh of the child waxed warm. Then he returned, and walked in the house to and fro; and went up, and stretched himself upon him: and the child sneezed seven times, and the child opened his eyes. And he called Gehazi, and said, Call this Shunammite. So he called her. And when she was come in unto him, he said, Take up thy son. Then she went in, and fell at his feet, and bowed herself to the ground, and took up her son, and went out.
2 KINGS 4:16-37.

The Shunammite woman is one example of women in the Bible that received their dead back alive. She released her faith to defeat her hopeless situation – the death of her son. If you can do what she did, you can get what she got. Her story educates us about how we can use our faith to defeat a hopeless situation.

What did she do to see her dead son return to life?

1. *She did not announce the death*

According to verse 21 of the story, the woman put her dead son in the room and shut the door. She did not announce to the world what had happened. She did not confess the death of her son to other people. She did not accept that this was the end. She did not call a pity-party to wail and mourn. Announcing her son's death to the world would have been admitting that the devil had won. This would make the devil rejoice and feel good about the woman's sorrow.

This woman had an undefeated attitude. She showed her disapproval of the situation and refused in her heart to accept the death of her boy. This initiated her miracle.

As a believer, do not broadcast what the devil is doing in your life to the world. Do not spread a bad report about your situation around, if you know that you haven't finished exercising faith over that situation.

Faith does not acknowledge what the enemy is doing but what God is doing. For your faith to work in your situation, do not spread the news about it. Do not go from place to place, telling those who can't help you with your problem. Do not give any sign of admitting defeat in your situation. If you accept a problem, it will not respond to your faith.

Therefore, to release your faith to defeat your hopeless situation, do not accept that the situation is hopeless, and do not spread the bad news about it.

2. *She did not bury her dead*

The woman refused to bury her son. This meant that she had not lost all hope, despite knowing that life had departed from the child. She wasn't denying the reality of the situation; she was accepting the reality of God. The woman couldn't claim that she was expecting her dead child to live again if she went ahead with burying him.

This means that she really believed that it was still possible for the dead child to come back to life, so she had no need to bury him. Your faith can revive any dead situation, provided you have not buried the situation in your heart. In other words, you keep hope alive irrespective of the size or seriousness of the situation. Never lose all hope. Do not close the gate of your heart against possibility. Keep hoping and start releasing your faith into the situation.

3. She went to a place where help was available

The woman went to a man of God for help. Her faith made her remember the man of God. Your problem is almost solved if you can locate where the solution can be found.

It is part of exercising faith that you consult a man or woman of God for spiritual assistance concerning your situation. Sometimes, your faith alone can't bring the expected result, so you must be wise enough, and humble enough, to ask for help. That's what Christian brothers and sisters are for.

Sometime, you need the faith of someone else to succeed in your situation, especially if you are as emotionally challenged by a situation as this woman must have been. Faith in God makes you turn to God's people for help. We are not on our own in the kingdom, we are part of the Body of Christ.

But you mustn't turn to just anyone for help. If you are operating in faith, you must realise that it is only like-minded people – people with the same faith as you – that can be of help in certain challenges of life. If you want somebody to join you in trusting God for miracle, you will need to go to someone whose faith you trust.

Like-minded people of faith can help your faith to remain alive and active. So if you think you need help to defeat your hopeless situation, seek the advice and prayers of those who have faith – and if possible those that have stronger faith than yourself.

4. She maintained her good confession

According to verses 23 and 26, the Shunammite woman said, *"It shall be well"* and then, *"It is well."*

Despite the hopeless appearance of the situation, she maintained her confession of faith – in fact, it strengthened from 'it will happen' to 'it is happening'. She believed that all was well with the dead child. She never said that her child was dead. She did not allow the situation to dictate to her what to say, but allowed her faith in God to dictate her words.

For your faith to work, you will need to maintain your confession of faith, irrespective of how long ago the incident happened. Do not let your trouble put words into your mouth. Let the written word of God put words into your mouth concerning your situation – because there is always hope with God. Irrespective of the complications of the situation, keep on speaking the word of faith to it.

If you desire that a dead situation or person should come to life again, you will need to continue to speak the word of life to that situation and not the word of death. Speaking the word of hope to your hopeless situation will turn things around in the direction you desire.

5. She did not rest until she received her dead son alive

On her way to see the man of God, she did not stop until she got to him. And she did not rest on the way back either. She did not allow any delay. This is wisdom generated by faith. Faith in God generates the necessary wisdom that creates a conducive environment for faith to thrive.

Faith requires that you do not rest until you have your result. Speed and time are important if certain miracles in life are to take place. If you want your situation to change, it may mean not wasting time. Passion is part of the evidence of faith. If you are operating in faith, you will need to get rid of procrastination. This is because it allows distractions to get in the way. Do not rest until your faith changes the situation that looks hopeless. Maintain the momentum of faith over that situation. Do not give the problem any time to worsen. Keep on the fight until that situation turns around.

6. She was persistent

2 KINGS 4:30 shows that she refused to leave the man of God. She hung onto Elisha until she obtained her miracle. Faith is persistence. You will need to continually apply faith to your situation, until you obtain the result you desire. A request that keeps on coming to God will one day receive favourable attention. Persistence is an indication that you are not ready to give up nor compromise your expectations.

Your persistence reveals your desperation. A desperate man can't be shouted down. Furthermore, your persistence is an indication that you have no other god to trust for your miracle. That is, it is either God or nothing. That is faith. This attitude of faith releases your faith into the situation so that a miracle can happen.

7. She ruled over tradition

In 2 KINGS 4:23, the husband of the woman reminded her that it was neither a new moon nor a Sabbath day, so why go to the man of God now? This is legalism. It must have been a tradition that people only went to see the man of God on certain days, not just any time. Unfortunately, the death of the boy did not occur at a convenient time, so the woman was in danger of losing her miracle if she kept to tradition. But the woman refused to respect the kind of tradition that hindered a miracle.

If you want to exercise your faith over a situation of your life, you must identify those general beliefs and norms that hinder miracles in your society. Do not allow the traditions of the world to get in the way of your faith. If exercising your faith is not welcome among the people around you, you must refuse to surrender your faith. The faith that defeats a hopeless situation must exalt God above every tradition of mankind.

8. She walked by faith

According to 2 CORINTHIANS 5:7, *"we walk by faith not by sight…"*

This woman walked by faith not by sight. She saw her child was dead, but by faith it was well with her child. Her actions were not determined by what she saw but by what she knew about the God who had removed the barrenness from her life in the beginning.

If you want to receive your dead alive or defeat your hopeless situation, you will need to walk by faith, not by sight. Do not rationalise the situation. Do not reason out the solution to your prevailing situation. You will need to refuse to be influenced by what you see but by what you know that your God can do for you. Be influenced by the Word of God, not by the word of man. Be directed by what you believe, not by what the world is showing you.

LUKE 1:37 says that *"with God nothing shall be impossible"*.

Faith in God has no limitations. There is no problem too big that faith in God can't solve. There is no situation too complex that faith in God can't handle. Faith in God can remove poverty, heal sickness both curable and incurable, change failure to success, make a way where there seems to be no way and do whatever seems impossible to man. It is a limitless faith.

Using Your Faith to Win Where Others Have Failed

CHAPTER 11

> *"I can do all things through Christ which strengtheneth me."*
>
> PHILIPPIANS 4:13

You can release your faith to win where other people have failed. By faith, it is possible to bring victory where before there was only defeat.

There are situations in life where you want to attempt what other people have tried and failed. Sometimes, you want to choose a career that other people have entered but have been unsuccessful. Or it may be that you want to start a business that other people have started but have gone out of business. But by faith, it is possible for you to succeed where others have not. By faith, you can win a battle that other people have run away from. By faith, it is possible for you to thrive on a path other people have turned away from.

CASE STUDY: DAVID AND GOLIATH

"And he stood and cried unto the armies of Israel, and said unto them, Why are ye come out to set your battle in array? am not I a Philistine, and ye servants to Saul? choose you a man for you, and let him come down to me. If he be able to fight with me, and to kill me, then will we be your servants: but if I prevail against him, and kill him, then shall ye be our

servants, and serve us. And the Philistine said, I defy the armies of Israel this day; give me a man, that we may fight together. When Saul and all Israel heard those words of the Philistine, they were dismayed, and greatly afraid." 1 SAMUEL 17:8-11

In this story, Goliath challenged the nation of Israel to battle but nobody was bold enough to confront him. Everybody, including King Saul, was afraid. But a small boy called David rose against Goliath to fight him. David chose to fight a battle everyone ran away from. Eventually, David won where everyone else had failed. David defeated Goliath by faith.

This chapter will show you how you can emulate David to release your faith to win where other people have failed.

Let us see how David won the battle everybody was afraid of.

1. David had the perspective of faith

David saw the situation from a different direction. He did not accept the negative situation that others did.

We can see this in 1 SAMUEL 17:24-27:

> *"And all the men of Israel, when they saw the man, fled from him, and were sore afraid. And the men of Israel said, Have ye seen this man that is come up? surely to defy Israel is he come up: and it shall be, that the man who killeth him, the king will enrich him with great riches, and will give him his daughter, and make his father's house free in Israel. And David spake to the men that stood by him, saying, What shall be done to the man that killeth this Philistine, and taketh away the reproach from Israel? for who is this uncircumcised Philistine, that he should defy the armies of the living God? And the people answered him after this manner, saying, So shall it be done to the man that killeth him."*

The Israelites looked into the situation from Goliath's side, believing he would be unbeatable in battle, while David was interested in the opportunity side. When David heard about the rewards of defeating Goliath, he saw the situation from the victory side and was not put off by the size of the task because he believed God was more powerful than any giant.

The opportunities awaiting David if he defeated Goliath gave him motivation to fight the battle. Motivation boosts faith, and then faith will move the person into action. But when you focus on the enormity of the problem, it will demotivate you and this will hinder your faith. Many people have failed in life because they focused on the difficulty of the challenges they needed to overcome in order to have success. Such people are more frightened by the big obstacles than excited by the big blessings that follow the victory.

Failure sees impossibility in all things, but success sees opportunities. A sense of impossibility hinders faith. But knowledge of what can be achieved breeds the motivation that boosts faith.

David discovered that defeating Goliath would benefit him and all his family. He knew that if he defeated Goliath, he would marry the king's daughter and become a royal family member; he would have great riches and his father's house would no longer pay taxes. In David's eyes, the rewards were worth the risks.

If you want to succeed where others have failed, you must focus on the gains and opportunities awaiting you. Don't focus on the challenges to overcome but the level of opportunities. Think about how your life and that of your family will be transformed when you succeed. If that motivates you, then it will boost your faith and move you into taking action in line with your faith. Focus on the opportunities, not the size of the obstacles.

Remember the word of God in PHILIPPIANS 4:13: *"I can do all things through Christ which strengtheneth me."*

You can win battles others have lost.

2. David used the method of faith

David faced Goliath with a different method which was born of his faith. Perhaps he reasoned that if soldiers who knew the conventional methods of warfare were too afraid to face Goliath, then no conventional method would work. Only a method based on faith could do the job.

> *"And Saul armed David with his armour, and he put an helmet of brass upon his head; also he armed him with a coat of mail. And David girded his sword upon his armour, and he assayed to go; for he had not proved it. And David said unto Saul, I cannot go with these; for I have not proved them. And David put them off him."*
> 1 SAMUEL 17:38-39

Saul gave David conventional armour to wear in the fight against Goliath, but David refused it. David probably reasoned that if Saul's armour could give the victory, why did Saul not use it to face Goliath?

David chose to do things differently. He used a method of faith that God had taught him in the past: *"And he took his staff in his hand, and chose him five smooth stones out of the brook, and put them in a shepherd's bag which he had, even in a scrip; and his sling was in his hand: and he drew near to the Philistine"* (1 SAMUEL 17:40).

David chose five small stones to face a giant that soldiers with better weapons of warfare had failed to confront. This implies that David had chosen to put his confidence in God for victory, not just a different weapon. He chose to trust God instead of man. This kind of faith can't be defeated because it depends totally on God.

His faith came from experience. With God's help, he had killed wild animals with his sling before, while protecting the sheep.

If you want to win where others have failed, you have to do things differently by putting your trust totally in God. Trust in what He has done for you and others in the past. That is faith that will always win.

3. David had conviction of faith

Your conviction is a strong belief that so governs your decisions that you are willing to die for it. David had a conviction totally different from other people.

King Saul and the other soldiers believed that they needed a very experienced fighter to defeat Goliath, whereas David was just an inexperienced youth: *"And Saul said to David, Thou art not able to go against this Philistine to fight with him: for thou art but a youth, and he a man of war from his youth"* (1 SAMUEL 17:33).

Saul was relying on a conviction that arose from his own experience and knowledge. But David had a different conviction about the matter: *"And David spake to the men that stood by him, saying, What shall be done to the man that killeth this Philistine, and taketh away the reproach from Israel? for who is this uncircumcised Philistine, that he should defy the armies of the living God?"* (1 SAMUEL 17:26).

David called Goliath an uncircumcised person – a recognition that Goliath had no covenant with the God of Israel. David's conviction was that the winner would be the one that had a covenant relationship with God.

So David believed that he could defeat Goliath, not because of his experience in warfare or his own strength, but because he was a child of the covenant. This is a conviction of faith.

Your conviction determines your attitude to the situations of life. People lose battles in life because they have the wrong convictions.

If you want to win battles others have lost, develop a conviction of faith. Believe that victory will come because you are a child of the new covenant. As a child of covenant you have the backing of heaven in all your battles. When this conviction is rooted in your heart, it boosts your faith so that you can see yourself victorious in any battle.

4. David had the drive of faith

'Drive' means the force that is controlling your actions. Your drive is your motive behind your actions. Your drive will determine your approach to a situation. If your drive is carnal (selfish), your approach will be carnal, and if it is spiritual your approach will be of faith.

In 1 SAMUEL 17:26, David asks who is this Philistine "that he should defy the armies of the living God?" David is driven by his love for God and a passion for God to be honoured. He can't stand anybody insulting his God. He loves God so much that he is ready to fight Goliath to protect the good name of God. That is his drive.

People fail in life mostly because they have the wrong drive or motive behind their actions. If you want to win where others have failed, develop a drive of faith. Let your purpose be to honour God. This will generate the fire of faith inside of you that will keep on pushing you forward, without being afraid of the difficulty of the challenges.

Please be aware that your faith in God can't work for you when your purpose is carnal: selfish motives will lead you to glorify man instead of God. For example, your faith in God will not produce results if your drive is materialism, envy, ego or other things of the flesh.

5. David had a vision of faith

Vision is about your goal – what you believe and expect to be the outcome. It is about what you desire to achieve at the end of the mission.

David had a vision of faith that was totally different from the people around him. His vision was to show the world that his God was real and was in charge of all things: *"This day will the LORD deliver thee into mine hand; and I will smite thee, and take thine head from thee; and I will give the carcases of the host of the Philistines this day unto the fowls of the air, and to the wild beasts of the earth; that all the earth may know that there is a God in Israel"* (1 SAMUEL 17:46).

David wanted the name of God to be exalted among all the nations. His intention was for his defeat of Goliath to demonstrate to the world that Israel's God was to be feared and worshipped. That was the vision he wanted to be fulfilled and the goal he set out to achieve at the end of the battle.

Some believers have claimed that they used their faith on a certain mission but it did not bring the expected result. The answer may be that the vision was ungodly. Faith in God only responds to the things of God. So do not be afraid to fight a battle that some other people have lost, because it could be that they lost because they were following an ungodly vision.

The vision of faith is a vision that is of God and not of man. When you release your faith on things that are of God, the situation has no choice but to respond to you favourably. To win where others have failed, ensure that your vision aligns with the Word of God, will advance the kingdom of God and will touch other lives.

6. David relied on his past experience of faith

David relied not on his experience of the battlefield but on his experience of defending his sheep. He chose to use the experience God had taught him in the journey of life.

> *"And Saul said to David, Thou art not able to go against this Philistine to fight with him: for thou art but a youth, and he a man of war from his youth. And David said unto Saul, Thy servant kept his father's sheep, and there came a lion, and a bear, and took a lamb out of the flock: and I went out after him, and smote him, and delivered it out of his mouth: and when he arose against me, I caught him by his beard,*

> *and smote him, and slew him. Thy servant slew both the lion and the bear: and this uncircumcised Philistine shall be as one of them, seeing he hath defied the armies of the living God."* (1 SAMUEL 17:33-36)

Saul thought that only those with many years of experience in fighting battles could defeat Goliath, but David proved him wrong. David believed that the battle would only be won by the man that God had prepared in His own time. David relied on his past experience of faith.

Do not forget the lessons God has taught you on the journey of life. God has given you certain experiences in the past to boost your faith. If God has delivered you before, He is able to deliver you again and again. To win where other people have failed, recall your past experience and encounters of faith. This will boost your faith and release it into action.

Whenever you face a new situation, check your past and you will discover that God has been preparing you for certain things in life. Your friends or relatives might have failed in certain things they did because they had not been prepared for it, whereas you might have been prepared for it. If that's the case, then you have an advantage that they didn't have.

7. *David had an attitude of faith*

Your attitude is the way you see a situation and behave towards it. David faced Goliath with an attitude of faith. He chose just five small stones to fight Goliath: *"And he took his staff in his hand, and chose him five smooth stones out of the brook, and put them in a shepherd's bag which he had, even in a scrip; and his sling was in his hand: and he drew near to the Philistine"* (1 SAMUEL 17:40).

But what is the possible reason for David choosing such stones?

No doubt it's because they were the same sort of stones that he had used to kill the lion and the bear. He also knew that, in close combat,

Goliath's strength would prevail, so with a sling, he could keep his distance and attack Goliath without having to get too near to his weapons. And the size of Goliath made him a big target, so David knew he could hit him with the stones.

Unfortunately, Saul and the other Israelites thought that Goliath's height was a threat to whoever fought him, but to David, it only made Goliath an easy target.

To defeat a big problem, David used a small solution – but his attitude was key. His attitude was positive, not negative, because He believed that God was on his side.

If you want to win battles other people have lost, you will need an attitude of faith. Faith is always positive – because with faith you realise that your God is always bigger than your enemy. This will release your faith into action.

8. David saw Goliath already defeated before the fight began

> *"This day will the LORD deliver thee into mine hand; and I will smite thee, and take thine head from thee; and I will give the carcases of the host of the Philistines this day unto the fowls of the air, and to the wild beasts of the earth; that all the earth may know that there is a God in Israel."* 1 SAMUEL 17:46.

When David faced Goliath, he saw a walking corpse standing in front of him. David declared to Goliath that he would take his head from him that very day. David was not using words like 'if' or 'maybe' or 'probably'. He was categorically stating what would definitely happen. There was no hesitation in his word.

He was not boasting or being overconfident. He simply had faith that because he was doing the right thing, God would fight his battle, and God never loses. David believed that any battle God allows His children to face has already been won before the battle has begun. So, to David, for God to have allowed him to face Goliath in battle, the battle must have already been won for him by God.

While all Israelites, including King Saul, were seeing the impossibility of defeating Goliath, David saw Goliath already defeated.

The Apostle Paul wrote: *"There hath no temptation taken you but such as is common to man: but God is faithful, who will not suffer you to be tempted above that ye are able; but will with the temptation also make a way to escape, that ye may be able to bear it"* (1 CORINTHIANS 10:13).

This confirms that God will not let you face a situation that is beyond your strength to endure. This implies that any battle or challenges that come your way are winnable, and that is why God allows them. They may not all be over as quick as David's battle, but God's timing is always perfect. Therefore, you will need to see your enemy already defeated and approach the situation with that belief and confidence. You need to see yourself winning that battle other people have lost, no matter how long it takes.

9. David leaned on grace

Some people fail in life because they lean only on their own experience and expertise. Unfortunately, when all their attributes have proved ineffective, they surrender.

David chose five smooth stones to fight Goliath. Numbers in the Bible often have spiritual significance. Spiritually, five means grace. Indirectly, David's faith was telling him that this battle would only be won by God's grace and not by any personal attributes or human qualifications.

When faith comes into operation, it brings grace along. Grace means divine favour that we don't deserve – it is God's gift to us. It sustains a believer to face and pass through any difficult or challenging situation. Grace qualifies the unqualified. It makes the weak overcome the mighty. Every little effort of a person who has received grace can yield mighty results. Ordinary weapons in the hand of a person who has received grace are mightier than stronger weapons in the hand of a warrior.

When you lean on grace, you see yourself as stronger than you are and you see your little effort as mightier than its normal power. To win where other people have failed in life will require that you lean on grace. That is, believe that victory is not going to be by human power only, but by God's hand upon the one He has chosen to favour. Therefore, with that faith in His grace, your little effort can still win that battle.

10. David had the passion of faith

> *"And it came to pass, when the Philistine arose, and came, and drew nigh to meet David, that David hastened, and ran toward the army to meet the Philistine."* (1 SAMUEL 17:48)

David ran to the battle! He was not sluggish. He did not fight like somebody who had reluctantly been persuaded to fight. He had self-motivation for what he was doing. He did not wait for anybody to persuade or encourage him. The fire of faith was burning intensely inside of him. All that was moving him into action was inside. He was not waiting for a human push.

Faith that will win where other people have failed will need to be passionate about what it is doing. Passion generates an internal fire that energises the person of faith. People fail in life due to lack of passion. Where there is no passion, there will be no internal fire and there will be no internal energy to activate the spirit to generate actions of faith. Be a believer that does everything with a holy passion.

Releasing the Creative Power of Faith into Action

CHAPTER 12

> *"We having the same spirit of faith, according as it is written, I believed, and therefore have I spoken; we also believe, and therefore speak..."*
>
> 2 Corinthians 4:13

Faith is creative. When faith gets to a place where there seems to be no way, faith creates a way. When faith comes across a stubborn situation that defies all solutions, it comes up with an alternative solution. Faith never gives up. Faith allows you to think outside the box, which results in innovative or different approaches to a particular task. This helps you to discover a new way of solving a problem when the normal ways fail. There is no hindrance or obstacles that faith can't overcome. Living faith is undefeatable.

This chapter will show you how to release your faith into motion by refusing to give up on a task that is hindered by obstacles.

We shall consider one biblical example where faith creates a way in order to overcome obstacles.

CASE STUDY: THE WOMAN OF THE ISSUE OF BLOOD

"And a certain woman, which had an issue of blood twelve years, and had suffered many things of many physicians, and had spent all that she had, and was nothing bettered, but rather grew worse, when she had heard of

Jesus, came in the press behind, and touched his garment. For she said, if I may touch but his clothes, I shall be whole. And straightway the fountain of her blood was dried up; and she felt in her body that she was healed of that plague." MARK 5:25-29.

In this story a woman with a constant haemorrhage came to Jesus for healing. Unfortunately, there was a large crowd around Jesus that prevented the woman from reaching Jesus. At this stage, the only credible option left for her was to return home and try again another time. But instead of giving up, the seed of faith inside her devised a solution to overcome the hindrance. She stretched her hand through the crowd until she touched the hem of Jesus' garment. She was healed instantly, despite the fact that Jesus did not pray for her.

Faith never surrenders to obstacles. With faith, there will always be a way. When you choose not to surrender to a problem, you will set in motion the power of faith to create ideas and means of beating the obstacles. Faith creates a way where there seems to be no way. Faith never surrenders to road-blocks. Faith can create an unusual means of solving a problem when the usual way seems blocked. If you can refuse to accept defeat, your faith will give you the inspiration and resources to overcome the obstacles that stand in your way.

But how did the woman create a conducive environment in her heart that enabled a seed of faith within her to influence her reaction to the obstacle?

1. She believed the report of faith she heard about Jesus

The Bible says that she heard that Jesus was in town. Probably the person that told her that Jesus could help would have told her about certain things that Jesus had done. When you hear a report of faith like that, and believe it, it will boost the faith you already had in your spirit.

2. She ministered faith to herself

The woman told herself that if she could just touch his clothes, she would be healed. By making such a confession of faith, she had prepared herself for healing. Therefore, the whole of her body was waiting for healing. There was nothing inside her that was contrary to her healing at this stage. Even her mind had one direction. There was no internal division within her. If you are going to overcome obstacles, you will need to minister faith to yourself. You must silence any contrary thoughts in your mind when you come against any hindrance on the way.

3. She took into consideration the possibility of hindrance

She said 'if' she may touch the clothes of Jesus. She knew it would be difficult to reach Jesus, as there was such a big crowd and he was so popular. But she had prepared herself for any eventuality. At this stage of her faith, it had become impossible for any surprising situation to hinder her. Many people give up at the point of hindrance because they never thought there would be a hindrance. So when they come across an obstacle in their path, they easily give up. But real faith is unstoppable. Real faith recognises that there will be opposition to anything good, but is not afraid of any hindrance. Real faith expects resistance from the enemy and is ready to subdue any opposition or aggression from him. To prepare yourself to overcome any hindrance, you will need to take into consideration the possibility of resistance from the enemy. This takes your faith above any surprises.

4. She was resolute

The woman had already made several failed attempts to find healing by consulting physicians, but despite all her past failures, she refused to give up. She had in her spirit, the kind of faith that is determined not to give up. So coming across a crowd in her way was no surprise but neither was it going to deter her. She was already in the position of faith that believes any obstacle can be overcome. For your faith to be victorious, you will need to be a resolute believer. Remember, when you come across an obstacle, that what you have already instilled inside your spirit will come alive. Regularly feed your faith with spiritual nutrients, so that on the day your faith comes across a mighty mountain, it will bring out a means to overcome.

5. She came to Jesus with strong expectations

The woman had already told herself that she would be made whole. This implies that her body, soul and spirit were all waiting for her healing. Strong expectation has a strong will behind it. When such a will comes across any opposition, it will not surrender but seek the way to defeat it. If you want your faith to create a way for you to overcome a hindrance to your miracle, make your expectation strong; develop a strong will that is undefeatable.

6. She simplified the process

The woman believed that merely touching the clothes of Jesus would be enough for her to be healed. Her faith was so strong that she believed Jesus did not need to touch her nor have any encounter with her before she would be healed. She had been ill for a very long time, but that didn't stop her believing that she could be healed in an instant. Faith in God is not complicated or sophisticated. You do not need church rituals or theological training or years of experience for faith to be effective. In fact, our intellect can sometimes get in the way of our faith, if it causes doubt and uncertainty. Nothing will be able to hinder your faith if you simplify the process in your heart, by simply believing that just one touch from Jesus is enough to give you a miracle.

7. Her actions backed up her faith

Speaking and confessing your faith will not be enough in some situations. Sometime you will need to take some action and apply some effort in order to get your miracle. Such faith easily overcomes obstacles. When you put in the work to back up your faith, your faith creates a means for you to overcome anything that would stop you.

Faith is creative. When faith comes across an obstacle that prevents its advancement, instead of giving up, it creates a way round, or a way over. But it is important to know that you will need to position your spirit in a certain way that will enable your faith to become creative whenever it comes across any hindrance. Fresh ideas will come from the depth of your spirit to enable you to navigate around an obstacle, if you ensure that your actions work in union with your faith. It is when you refuse to quit that you will experience your faith arising. With faith, there is no situation you can't defeat. Faith takes over at the face of hindrance to pave a way for advancement. Faith in God is a spiritual gift, given to you by His Holy Spirit when you became a Christian, and it resides inside your inner being. It can generate inside of you any action that is needed to overcome any hindrance.

Like the woman who suffered from bleeding, we need to get our spirit ready to unleash the creative power of faith when we come across a hindrance. Here are some ways in which we can do that.

1. Maintain the tempo

As you travel on the journey of faith, don't lose your passion. Maintain the speed, the pace, the momentum that your faith has generated inside of you. Let nothing intimidate you. Keep the fire of faith burning inside of you. Keep on feeding your faith with spiritual nutrients such as thanksgiving, praise, confession of the Word of God, hope, prayer, etc. Such a faith will not let you give in to opposition.

Paul told Timothy to 'stir up' the gift within him: *"Wherefore I put thee in remembrance that thou stir up the gift of God, which is in thee by the putting on of my hands"* (2 TIMOTHY 1:6).

It is our responsibility to build up our faith, so that it will enable us to stand against any hindrance in the future. If you do this, you will be able to call upon your faith when you need it to defeat any obstacles in your way.

Do not conform to the dictates of the situation, but instead, maintain your confession, your passion, your hope, your confidence and your expectation of what God will do, irrespective of the challenges. This will position you to enjoy the creative power of faith when your own ideas are exhausted in the face of a hindrance.

2. Refuse to quit

Keep on trying! If you refuse to quit, your faith will birth in you, a solution to the challenges. Those who keep on searching for the way will definitely find it. When you refuse to quit, your faith will rise up inside of you to bring you the way forward.

1 Corinthians 16:13 tells us to *"stand fast in the faith… be strong."* If you refuse to throw in the towel and remain strong in faith, God will show you the way to overcome the enemy.

3. Refuse to accept that there is no other way forward

In the face of strong opposition, sometimes your senses tell you that there is no other way forward and that it is better to quit now. But if you can refuse to accept such negative suggestions, you will position your spirit to be influenced by your faith to create a way for you. Failure believes that there is only one way of doing things, and that way is the one he has tried that did not work. But success believes that there must be another way to victory. Such positive belief prepares you for the creativity of faith.

Isaiah 42:16 says: *"And I will bring the blind by a way that they knew not; I will lead them in paths that they have not known: I will make darkness light before them, and crooked things straight. These things will I do unto them, and not forsake them."*

This verse shows that God knows the way ahead when we don't. There is a way no one has thought of but Him. When you have tried all the ways you know and they have not worked, expect God to show you the way you did not know. This will happen only if you have not closed the gate of your mind by saying that there is no other way forward.

4. Strengthen your will power

There is a common saying that where there is a will there is a way. There is a lot of truth in this. The strength of your will power will greatly influence your resolution.

> *"The woman was a Greek, a Syrophenician by nation; and she besought him that he would cast forth the devil out of her daughter. But Jesus said unto her, Let the children first be filled: for it is not meet to take the children's bread, and to cast it unto the dogs. And she answered and said unto him, Yes, Lord: yet the dogs under the table eat of the children's crumbs."* MARK 7:26-28

In this story, a woman came to Jesus for her daughter to be healed. Jesus intentionally took her through a process that would test her faith. But what He said did not discourage the woman. She persisted in her request and in the end, it was granted. Her will power could not be broken by Jesus' objection that His mission was to the people of Israel first. When your will power is unbreakable and remains strong despite all the discouraging things that come your way, then your faith will create a way for you where it seemed there was no way.

5. Avoid tradition

Tradition says that things can only be done the way they have always been done, and that is the end of the matter. This means that if the old way of doing things fails, then there is nothing that can be done but to surrender. But with faith, there is always a way. It may be that you don't know another way, but nothing is impossible for God. If the old way fails, a new way will work. In faith, the same miracle can happen many times – but in different ways.

In MARK 7:13, Jesus said scolded the Pharisees for *"making the word of God of none effect through your tradition, which ye have delivered: and many such like things do ye."*

If tradition clashes with the Word of God, then tradition must go. It will not allow the creative power of your faith to be unleashed. To enjoy the power of your faith, you will need to open up your spirit to fresh ideas, especially when the old ones fail.

6. All things will work together for your good

When you get to the point where it seems that there is no way forward, stand on the Word of God that promises that all things will work together for your good: *"And we know that all things work together for good to them that love God, to them who are the called according to his purpose"* (ROMANS 8:28).

"All things" include both the good and the bad, the known and the unknown. Faith believes that something will happen in its favour, though, it does not know what that will be.

7. Speak out your expectations to the situation

Faith responds to words. When you speak out your expectations, irrespective of the prevailing negative situation around you, your faith gets into action to work in fulfilment of your word. Suddenly, the veil of impossibility that covers your understanding will fall off and fresh ideas will come.

2 CORINTHIANS 4:13 shows the important relationship between our faith and our words: *"We having the same spirit of faith, according as it is written, I believed, and therefore have I spoken; we also believe, and therefore speak…"*

Speak out your belief, not what the situation presents to you. Speak out deliverance in a situation where all effort to bring deliverance has failed. In a situation where you have searched for a job many times before with no success, speak out that you will get a new job. Speak out healing when all efforts to be healed have failed. Verbalise your expectation, turn it into words of faith.

8. Never justify failure

If you want your faith to create a way forward in the face of challenge and hindrance, don't accept reasons for failure.

While it may seem that failure is imminent, still don't believe that there is a reason for failure. If your first attempt failed, don't draw a conclusion to justify failure. Instead, try again and again and again until you succeed. When you hit a wall, don't accept that there is no way round it. Avoid making negative conclusions about your situation, because negative conclusions produce negative attitudes in you.

For example, in NUMBERS 13 and 14, when the Israelites said that they couldn't fight the Amalekites because they were so huge, they developed a negative attitude towards Moses and those who were positive among them.

Negative conclusions produce negative attitudes, and they will not allow your faith to be released into your situation.

9. Face your reality from the exact opposite direction

For your faith to move you forward when you are confronting a negative situation, you will need to choose to be different from the prevailing situation. You will need to operate in the opposite direction to your prevailing situation.

For example, you will need to be positive, however negative your situation. If you choose to be negative in a negative situation, your faith will be locked up inside of you. You will need to do things differently in order to release your faith and enable you to climb over that wall standing before you. Face coldness with warmness. Be friendly in a hostile environment. Face impossibility with a possibility mindset. Face bad news with good news. Be calm in the face of restlessness. Maintain order when you face disorder.

This response activates your faith and suddenly you receive a way forward.

Attributes of Faith

CHAPTER 13

"My counsel shall stand, and I will do all my pleasure ...I have spoken it, I will also bring it to pass; I have purposed it, I will also do it."

ISAIAH 46:10-11

In this chapter we will look into the attributes that faith exhibits as it faces different situations in life. Faith that will always win must exhibit these attributes.

1. Faith is fully persuaded

Genuine faith in Jesus is fully persuaded, totally convinced that God will do what He has promised in His word.

ROMANS 4:20-21 shows that Abraham, despite being advanced in age, was certain that God not only could, but would do what He promised. He was fully persuaded. If you are completely convinced about a promise of God, you will not waiver between two opinions, such as: "Will God do it or not?" A fully persuaded faith has only one opinion, which is: the Lord will do as He has promised.

2. Faith sees beyond the natural

Faith in Jesus sees beyond what is happening in the natural world and instead puts its expectation in God. It believes in miracles – the situations where God suspends or circumvents the natural laws to achieve His purpose.

In GENESIS 22:7-8, when Isaac asked Abraham about the lamb for sacrifice, Abraham replied by telling him that God would provide. Abraham had no clue how this would happen, but he chose to see beyond what the natural world was showing and focus on what God could do. Real faith in God believes that miracles can happen to fulfil the promises of God. Despite all the negativities around your expectations, God can still perform His word miraculously.

3. Faith is patient

Patience is the ability to endure and exercise perseverance and restraint. Genuine faith in God will patiently wait for God to keep His Word. Due to its patience, faith will not yield to the pressure of time, which tempts us to look for a shortcut. Real faith will wait for God's time.

HEBREWS 6:12 states that we inherit the promises *"through faith and patience"*. How long can you wait for God to fulfil His promise in your life? You will need to wait as long as it takes. This is because God has a time for everything He will do in your life, and since you are not sure of the exact time, wisdom dictates that you should wait until God does it – not try and force the situation yourself.

4. Faith is expectant

Genuine faith in God always looks forward towards the manifestation of God's promises. Faith does not just pray about a situation but expects God to be at work. PROVERBS 23:18 says that *"thine expectation shall not be cut off"*. Your expectation is a reflection of your confidence that God will fulfil your desires because those desires are in line with His Word. If you know God has promised it, expect it.

Attributes of Faith

Expectation also breeds preparation. What you expect to happen is what you will prepare for. For example, if you are trusting God for a child, prepare for children coming into your house. Make your house ready for the birth, so that your faith is not a matter of what you wish for but what you believe and expect.

5. Faith is consistent

Genuine faith is consistent. A person of faith continues in prayer, sacrifice, giving, fasting, serving God and every other act of faith he or she has been practising. Faith does not stop praying because its expectation fails to materialise. Irrespective of the prevailing negative circumstances, faith does not stop doing the right things. Genuine faith is constantly adhering to the same principles and practices. It holds firmly to God.

In 1 SAMUEL 1, Hannah kept on going to Shiloh to request a child from God. She kept on doing the same thing year by year, and never gave up until one day God answered her. Never stop doing the right things of faith because one day, there will be results.

6. Faith always praises God

Praise is an expression of thanksgiving to the Lord. You give praise to thank God for what He Has done in your life and for what He means to you. Faith does not hold praise back from God just because God has not done what you have been trusting Him to do.

Real faith keeps on thanking God, because He will do what He has promised He will do. When you give God a sacrifice of praise despite not seeing your answer to prayer, God is pleased. You cannot outgive God. Your praise provokes God to greater blessings, to go beyond your expectations.

Praise is powerful. In 2 CHRONICLES 20, the people of Judah cried out to God for deliverance from their strong enemies, and they gave

Him praise before their deliverance. God not only delivered them from the great armies ranged against them, but gave Judah the riches of their enemies. Whether your expectations have materialised or not, keep on thanking God by giving Him genuine and heartfelt praise. He is worth it.

7. Faith resists the devil

When faith comes across opposition to its trust in God, it rises against it. Real faith in God does not surrender to doubt sowed by the enemy or obstacles he puts in the way, but resists the devil and his schemes. JAMES 4:7 tells us that if we resist him, the devil will flee, which means that the devil is defeatable. Why? Because he was defeated at the cross. If you stand your ground and fight, the devil cannot win. When the devil sees that all that he is throwing at you to frustrate your faith doesn't stop you, he will leave you alone.

8. Faith stands on the counsel of God

Genuine faith stands on the counsel of God regarding the situations around it. Faith believes that, against all the odds, God's purposes will stand and what He says goes. If a man or woman of faith sees or hears negative things that are contrary to what they are expecting from God, that is not the time to given in. It is the time to prove that your faith in God is real and will not be moved.

Trust that God will keep His Word. In ISAIAH 46:10-11, God states: *"My counsel shall stand, and I will do all my pleasure... I have spoken it, I will also bring it to pass; I have purposed it, I will also do it."* What God has written concerning you will stand – not the opinions or reports of human beings.

9. Faith never draws back

HEBREWS 10:38 states that God has no pleasure in those believers who *"draw back"*. To draw back means to give up confidence in

Christ or to deny him. Some believers change their confession of faith due to the trials and temptations that come against their faith in God. Real faith never turns back. It never renounces God nor stops trusting in God's faithfulness, irrespective of the situation. Remember, it is not starting in faith that matters, but keeping on in faith and finishing in faith. Faith that will yield results must never draw back.

10. Faith demands results

Genuine faith in God does not pay attention to excuses that justify failure. It is only interested in results. Real faith in God keeps believing that God will come through for you.

In 1 KINGS 18:43-44, Elijah refused to accept the reports of no rain that his servant brought him. He kept sending his servant back to look for rain, again and again, until on the seventh occasion his servant told him that a tiny cloud appeared. Elijah took that cloud as the result he was looking for, and sure enough the rain came. Nothing pleases real faith except the expected result. If your faith is genuine, reasons for failure will never satisfy you. You will not be carried away by or distracted by the excuses for failure, but you will maintain an unshakable resolve until your 'cloud' appears.

11. Faith is irresistible

Genuine faith is so persistent that neither man nor God can fail to notice it, and God will give you what you ask because your persistence shows your faith. In his teaching on prayer, Jesus said that we should keep knocking at the door until the man inside gets up and opens the door (LUKE 11:5-10). He wasn't saying that God wants to ignore our pleas, and will only keep His promises if we irritate him so much that He says 'yes' in order to get rid of us. He was saying that persistence persuades God that we really mean business. God won't ignore your requests if you consistently stand on His Word.

Even if God decides not to answer your request because He knows what is best for you, He will still respond to you – either by giving you an explanation for His action or by giving you something better. In the Bible, all those who cried out to Jesus received His attention. In MARK 10:47-49, the cry of blind Bartimaeus was so strong and persistent that Jesus heard him and healed him. Real faith is irresistible. If you can keep the faith, you will be amazed how it will attract God's attention to your situation.

12. Faith is courageous

Courage is the strength you show in the face of pain, fear or danger. It gives you the ability to fight when it would be easier to give in. Genuine faith overpowers fear. Faith and fear do not go together. You can't have faith and still have fear. Faith is of God while fear is of the devil.

In 1 SAMUEL 17, despite the size, battle experience and weapons of Goliath, David was not afraid to confront him. David was so courageous that he did not allow the strength of Goliath to intimidate him. Real faith in God does not bow before intimidation or threats. If your faith is genuine, you should be courageous enough to advance in your trust in God despite all the danger and threats on the way.

13. Faith speaks the mind of God

When the spirit of a man is filled with faith in God, he operates with the mind of Christ. He speaks as God would speak in a situation. He makes a divine declaration about the situation. This is because faith in God gives you access to the mind of God and your spirit begins to see what your natural mind could not see. This is superimposed upon your spirit and printed on your mind. It determines your statements about the situation. You cannot operate by faith in God and still give voice to your own personal, human opinion on the issue.

Attributes of Faith

In EXODUS 14:13, Moses declared before Israel that the Egyptians they saw that day would never be seen again. As he declared, so God did. He spoke the mind of God. Check what you say regarding your situation; if it is not the mind of God, then you are not speaking in faith.

14. Faith stays positive

Even in difficulty and hardship, faith stays positive. Even when negatives seem the rational outcome, faith stays positive. In 2 KINGS 4:26, the Shunammite woman said all was well with her dead son. She stayed positive in a negative situation. The final result obeyed her position. Her dead child came alive. Real faith stays positive irrespective of the prevailing conditions and indications. The pendulum of faith will always finally swing to God's side, irrespective of the circumstances.

15. Faith rejoices always

Genuine faith in God has no bad day – every day is good because God is on our side. Negative situations cannot steal His joy from us. Bad news cannot steal His joy. Opposition or frustration cannot steal His joy. People of faith keep rejoicing whatever their circumstances.

In HABAKKUK 3:17-18, Habakkuk declares that he will keep on rejoicing despite the threat of famine around him. Clearly his joy does not depend on the circumstances of his life. It is made in heaven, not on earth. Faith in God is of heaven, not earth. Situations on the earth do not affect it. Faith that rejoices always will always end in joy. Keep on rejoicing irrespective of the outcome of your trust in God.

16. Faith celebrates victory before it appears

Faith believes that its answer is a settled matter before God; therefore, even before the manifestation of the answer, it is already celebrating. When an expected victory is celebrated, it seals up the victory. According to Jesus in MARK 11:24, whatever you pray for has been answered by God – if you believe it. This implies that after prayer, you are only waiting for the physical manifestation of the answer. If you believe that manifestation will certainly happen, you can start the celebration now. That is real faith in God.

17. Faith believes without seeing

In the world seeing is believing, but in faith, believing is seeing. In other words, unless you believe it you will not see it. In HEBREWS 11:13, heroes and heroines of faith saw the promises of God from afar, *"were persuaded of them, and embraced them"*. They saw into the future with the eyes of their mind. Genuine faith has eyes to see what ordinary eyes cannot see. That is why we can believe in something without seeing it physically. If your faith is genuine, you do not need to ask for or seek physical evidence before you can believe God to keep His promises in your life.

18. Faith is authoritative

A man of faith speaks authoritatively to the situation he is trusting God for. He uses a commanding tone against the situation – but it mustn't be an actor's voice, it must arise from the genuine belief that you have the authority that Christ has given you. People of faith exercise authority over situations that stand in their way. They control and order the situation as it pleases them. Words that will move heaven into action must be spoken with authority.

MATTHEW 7:29 states that Jesus spoke with authority. To make your faith effective will require that you speak with authority to the situations of your life.

19. Faith speaks repetitively

Faith in God speaks the same thing again and again until it is done. Faith in God does not change its beliefs according to the circumstances. It keeps on repeating itself until its word is

Attributes of Faith

established. As we have seen in 1 KINGS 18:43, Elijah kept on saying the same thing, giving the same word of instruction to his servant, until his expectation was established. If your faith is genuine, you do not need to change your word to accommodate the circumstances. Instead, you maintain your word to force the circumstances to conform to your word. Your word dictates what will happen, not the circumstances. That is faith in God.

20. Faith is full of hope

Faith in God is bursting with hope, always looking to the future, beyond the present situation. In times of poverty, faith looks to the future for abundance. In persecution, faith looks to the future for God's judgment. Faith in God is never destroyed by the prevailing negative situation. Faith is full of hope. It always hopes for the best from God. It hopes for divine intervention in its situation. ROMANS 8:24 states that *"we are saved by hope"*. Genuine faith in God never loses hope.

21. Faith sees Satan defeated

Even when it seems as if Satan is on the throne, reigning over the affairs of a believer, the person of faith sees Satan defeated. At the time it seems as if the problem is growing stronger, but faith in God maintains its belief that Satan was defeated many years ago when Jesus died on the cross for us. So, even when the enemy is still making threats, faith sees the enemy as a walking corpse, an empty barrel that makes the loudest noise. It sees the enemy defeated.

1 JOHN 5:4 states that our faith has overcome the world. This took place when Jesus died on the cross and rose again. Therefore, faith in God knows that the victory was settled 2,000 years ago when Jesus, *"having spoiled principalities and powers, he made a shew of them openly, triumphing over them in it"* (COLOSSIANS 2:15). Such a believer sees Satan as a defeated foe.

22. Faith steps out

Genuine faith takes a risk and steps out into the unknown. It doesn't settle for the familiar and easy. A faith-filled believer trusts that God will order his steps. Such a Christian believes that even if he sinks, his God will reach out to rescue him. He is not afraid of stepping out into the unknown.

In MATTHEW 14:28-31, Peter's faith enabled him to step out of the boat and walk on water. When he started sinking, Jesus stretched His hand out to save him. Genuine faith will not stay in the familiar due to fear of failure. How is your faith? Can you move forward into the future, trusting God to take you by the hand, lead you and uphold you?

23. Faith ignores the voice of reason

God has given you senses, such as sight, hearing, smell, touch and taste, to enable you to relate very well with the natural world. But our physical senses cannot be used to relate to the world of the supernatural. Faith is beyond the natural. Therefore faith can't operate by means of our physical senses.

In 2 KINGS 7:1-2, the servant of the king doubted that, after many years of famine, God could supply abundant food within 24 hours. His doubt was based on human reason. It was reasonable to suggest that farmers could not produce food from their farms in that time. But God is not limited by human reason! As a result of his cynicism, the servant saw the abundant food but he did not taste it. Genuine faith does not operate with human reasoning and senses. When your common sense tells you that your faith can't work, you will need to ignore it. Do not judge a situation with human reason when you are acting in faith. Follow God by spirit, not by flesh.

24. Faith calls things which are not as if they were

Genuine faith in God speaks about the promises of God that are yet to be fulfilled as if they were already accomplished. The man of faith shows the certainty of God's promises in his life. ROMANS 4:17 says that God *"calleth those things which be not as though they were"*. Real faith in God does not wait for a full manifestation of God's promises before it begins to walk in their certainty.

2 CORINTHIANS 1:20 has already declared that *"all the promises of God in him [Jesus] are yea, and in him Amen..."* That is, they are settled in heaven. If your faith is genuine, start treating those expectations of yours with certainty, even if they appear impossible. Plan and act according to your expectations not according to your present conditions. Live above your circumstances.

25. Faith speaks out

Faith in God is never silent and it can't be silenced. Even at the time of confrontation, faith in God speaks. In 1 SAMUEL 17:45-47, David spoke against Goliath as he faced him in battle. Before the stone of David hit the head of Goliath, the word of David had already position Goliath for defeat. Your word matters in faith. If your faith in God is real, then begin to speak your word of faith into your situation until the situation adjusts to your word.

26. Faith is calm

Faith in God is calm and settled. It exhibits peace. A man of faith does not lose his temper when faced with challenges. He remains calm and organised. He keeps himself under the control of the Holy Spirit in all situations.

If your faith in God is genuine, you should remain calm when you are in the middle of chaos. Faith enables you to release your burdens onto Jesus, and if this is the case, it should reflect in your calmness. In EXODUS 14:13-14, Moses was calm, despite seeing the Egyptians chasing the Israelites. He was calm because he saw God in the situation. How calm are you whenever you face challenges? Calmness enables you to hear from the Spirit of God that dwells inside of you.

27. Faith is obedient to God

Faith in God can't disobey God. If you are trusting God to fulfil His promises in your life, you can't be disobedient to the same God. The manifestation of your faith in God is evident by the level of your obedience. The more you obey God, the more the Word of God will work through you. When an obedient child of God speaks the Word of God, something will be accomplished.

PSALM 34:17 states that the Lord hears the cry of righteous. When an obedient child of God calls on God, He hears him. If the Word of God is not working for you, it could be due to your disobedience.

28. Faith leans on grace

Someone who has faith in God believes that God will release grace on him to perform the task that is too great for his natural ability. Such a man believes that he can do all things through Christ who strengthens him, as written in Philippians 4:13. Faith enables you to depend on the ability of God, not your own ability. If your faith is real, you should stop focusing on your limited strength to determine what you can or cannot do. Faith makes grace available.

29. Faith speaks the language of possibility in all situations

Genuine faith in God sees the possibilities in all things. What is impossible for human beings is possible with God (LUKE 1:37). If your faith is real, you should speak the language of possibility in all your challenges. To a person of faith, every mountain is conquerable and every Goliath is defeatable. A person of faith never runs away from battle. He believes all things are possible. He believes that his dreams can be achieved and that his plan can be carried out. If your faith is real, you should believe in possibility, irrespective of the level of the challenges.

Attributes of Faith

30. Faith claims its covenanted rights

As a believer, you are a child of the covenant. As such, you have certain rights in Jesus. HEBREWS 8:6 states that Jesus has brought us into a new and better covenant. That new covenant comes with certain benefits for those who follow Jesus, like healing, victory and prosperity. Faith in God gives you the right to claim those benefits. Genuine faith in God gives you the assurance that you have the right to claim those benefits.

31. Faith is active

Real faith in God is active, not passive. It generates momentum and positive action. It is very operational. It is driven by passion. You can't have faith in God and remain inactive. Inactive faith yields no results. 1 THESSALONIANS 1:3 talks about the *"work of faith"*. Faith produces work and it is this work that attracts the manifestation of your expectations. If you have faith then you should be at work. Faith in God is constantly doing something to attain its expectations.

32. Faith sticks to the original plan

In God, there is no alternative plan because the original plan can never fail. If your faith is genuine, you will not be heading anywhere but somewhere. Real faith does not keep on changing the plan and direction.

In Exodus 14, when Israel reached the Red Sea and there seemed to be no way forward, God did not give Israel an alternative route to the Promised Land. Instead, He made a way for them where there seemed to be no way. If your faith is real, you can't keep on changing your mind on what course to take. Real faith sticks to the original plan, and when challenges arise, it trusts God to remove the barriers.

33. Faith never bows

Genuine faith in God never bows to intimidation, harassment, fear, threats, discouragement, etc. In DANIEL 3:15-25, Shadrach,

Meshach and Abednego refused to bow to the threat of fire that the king set up to burn them. They maintained their faith in God. At the end of the story, their God arose for their deliverance. Faith never bows. Faith in God is firm and will never yield to a contrary situation, irrespective of the changing circumstances. If your faith is strong, you should not bow to a negative situation that the enemy is creating around you to force you to quit.

34. Faith speaks: there will be a performance

When genuine faith receives a word from God, it stands on it and continually declares that; that word will be fulfilled. In LUKE 1:45, when Elisabeth received a promise of God through Mary, she declared that there would be *"a performance"* or enactment of what God had promised. Shortly afterwards, it came true. The word of faith draws the promises of God into fulfilment. Whatever word you have received from God, be assured that it will be accomplished, irrespective of the hindrances or difficulties of your life. That is the faith that always wins.

Faith THAT ALWAYS WINS

Faith has been described as *"the substance of things hoped for, the evidence of things not seen"* (HEBREWS 11:1). This means that faith is the foundation on which all our hopes and convictions about the future are built.

This book will show you how to use the principles of faith to win in the battles of life. It helps you discover the promises in God's Word that will strengthen your faith and make you undefeatable in life. The whole content of this book has been tailored towards producing believers that will not be a push-over to the world, and that will access all that God has freely given to them by applying the principles of living faith in Him.

It is my prayer that as you read this book and put these principles into practice in the situations of your life, you will remain a winner through all your days – in Jesus' precious name.

About the Author

Fatai Kasali is a Pastor of the Redeemed Christian Church of God, Glory of God Parish, Bristol, England. He was trained as an engineer and was once a lecturer in a higher education institution.

God used him to establish Redeemed Christian Church of God, Glory of God Parish, in Lesotho, Southern Africa, and was later relocated to England. He is married to Felicia Ebunlomo and their glorious union is blessed with two sons.

BOOKS FROM THE SAME AUTHOR

Journey to the Next Level

The New Creature

Building a Glorious Home:
A Pathway to a Successful Marriage

The Winning Formula

The Enemy of Marriage

The Word that Heals

This book, and all other books from the same author, are available at Christian bookstores and distributors worldwide.

They can also be obtained through online retail partners such as Amazon or by contacting the author on the address below.

Contacts:

21-23 Stokescroft, Bristol, BS1 3PY

United Kingdom

E-mail:

kkasali@yahoo.com

Telephone:

+44 (0)7727159581

www.ingramcontent.com/pod-product-compliance
Lightning Source LLC
Chambersburg PA
CBHW070620300426
44113CB00010B/1602